Programmed Vocabulary

Second Edition
James I. Brown

Professor of Rhetoric
University of Minnesota

Prentice-Hall, Inc., Englewood Cliffs, New Jersey

ISBN: 0-13-730325-4

10

PRENTICE-HALL INTERNATIONAL, INC., *London*
PRENTICE-HALL OF AUSTRALIA, PTY. LTD., *Sydney*
PRENTICE-HALL OF CANADA, LTD., *Toronto*
PRENTICE-HALL OF INDIA PRIVATE LIMITED, *New Delhi*
PRENTICE-HALL OF JAPAN, INC., *Tokyo*

Contents

Preface

PROGRAMMED VOCABULARY is a programmed text providing a particularly useful shortcut to vocabulary development. Chief emphasis is placed on those basic principles and elements best calculated to speed vocabulary growth.

This book differs from other vocabulary texts in three important respects.

Programmed form

First, it is in programmed form. Some educators consider programmed instruction as the greatest forward step in education since the invention of movable type in the eleventh century.

All too often with a conventional book a reader finds himself slipping into a passive or semi-passive state when reading—into reading without really reading. To be sure, his eyes travel down the page. Only when he reaches the bottom of a page or the end of a section or chapter does he realize that his attention has wandered and that portions of the book are a complete blank. The programmed form does not permit such passive "reading." It demands an active written response at every step of the way. Obviously, fifteen minutes of active, concentrated learning are far better than hours of desultory study.

Every student knows how his attention rises to top pitch when he is actually called upon in class to recite. And every teacher has observed students change in an instant from passive listeners to active, alert responders in that situation. In a sense, the programmed approach capitalizes on this human characteristic. It is like having a private tutor by your side who, through a series of pointed questions, keeps your attention and interest high. In short, programming insures *active* participation.

Furthermore, programming is based on the principle of "errorless learning." Each step is so closely related to the preceding one that with reasonable concentration, mistakes are reduced to a minimum. If a wrong answer is made, it is corrected immediately before it has a chance to take root and become established.

The programmed form also capitalizes on what psychologists call *reinforcement,* thought by some to be the single most important factor in learning. It is the immediate checking of the right answer that serves to reinforce it. The more often this occurs and the sooner it follows the writing of a response, the better the learning.

Economy of learning

Second, this book is designed to teach much through little. There are two ways of learning something. It is possible, for example, to learn the meaning of fifty words and have that and no more to show for the effort. This text, however, is based on the belief that it is also possible to learn one thing in such a way as to learn forty-nine other things in the process.

In this text the numbered steps or frames, as they are called, are phrased so as to focus on the interrelationships upon which this extra learning dividend is based. Here, for example, is an actual frame from the unit on *inter-* which illustrates how the learner is led past the individual case to see and think in terms of the many.

When *pre-* is added to *empt* to make *preempt,* both *e*'s are retained. Similarly, when you add *inter-* to *racial,* should you write *interacial* or *interracial?*

Students in a university class were asked to spell twenty words before doing the short unit on *inter-*. Afterwards they were asked to spell the same twenty words. The first time through the spelling list the class members made ninety errors. After the programmed unit, they made only fifty-nine.

Although the purpose of the text is not to teach spelling, the class learned about *inter-* in such a way as to get a spelling dividend or bonus amounting to 34 percent improvement, thanks to the interrelationships stressed. Even greater dividends should be expected in the area of vocabulary, which receives major attention. Because of the applications and implications opened up, this book may well do more to accelerate learning than a conventional book two or three times its size.

Focus on basic elements and principles

This brings up a third difference. This text is built around basic language elements and principles.

For example, the carefully chosen language elements will acquaint you with words, a thousand at a time. The fourteen words to be studied contain prefix and root elements found in over 14,000 relatively common words or close to an estimated 100,000 of unabridged dictionary size.

As for basic principles, one is the principle of mnemonics, a most important

memory aid. Instead of a rote memorizing of the meanings of word elements, the
student is led to make associations which, in a sense, do his memorizing for him.

What does the prefix *hypo-* mean, for example? If you are not certain, here is
a frame to help you:

> To remember that *hypo-* means "under," think of where the doctor puts the
> _____ needle when he gives you a shot in the arm.

In this way the meaning of *hypo-* is almost memorized for you as you visualize the
gleaming hypodermic needle being pushed "under" your skin. As an added dividend, you see that *dermic* apparently refers to "skin."

Another basic principle is helpful in understanding language change—the important principle of *assimilation*. In frame after frame this concept is examined
and reinforced so as to bring a sharpened awareness of its operation.

For example, what do the following words have in common: *ascend, accept,
aggregate, ally, annex, append, arrive, assemble,* and *attract?* The uninitiated
would probably say, "They all begin with *a.*" Actually, all show the effects of assimilation, all containing assimilated forms of the prefix *ad-.*

Approximately 60 to 70 percent of the assimilative changes can be identified
through use of one key principle—the sign of the doubled consonant. This is
pointed up by such frames as this:

> To aid in spotting assimilative changes, remember *oppress, occlude,* and *offer.*
> In all three words the second and _____ letters are identical.

Other basic principles underlying the memorization, identification, and application of word parts are also stressed to insure maximum results. Finally, the reader
is led to use such principles to make generalizations covering hundreds of prefix
and root elements not specifically treated here.

II

The fourteen words

Instead of adding words to your vocabulary one at a time, here is a way of
getting acquainted with them a thousand at a time. Leonard A. Stevens, in a
Coronet article, calls them "The 14 Words That Make All the Difference."

They make all the difference because they contain the most useful shortcut
yet discovered to a bigger vocabulary. These fourteen words contain the twenty
most important prefixes and the fourteen most important roots—most important
because they are found in *over 14,000 words* of collegiate dictionary size or close
to an estimated 100,000 words of unabridged dictionary size.

Here they are:

The Fourteen Words

Keys to the meanings of over 14,000 words

DERIVATIONS

WORDS	PREFIX	COMMON MEANING	ROOT	COMMON MEANING
1. Precept	*pre-*	(before)	*capere*	(take, seize)
2. Detain	*de-*	(away, down)	*tenere*	(hold, have)
3. Intermittent	*inter-*	(between, among)	*mittere*	(send)
4. Offer	*ob-*	(against)	*ferre*	(bear, carry)
5. Insist	*in-*	(into)	*stare*	(stand)
6. Monograph	*mono-*	(alone, one)	*graphein*	(write)
7. Epilogue	*epi-*	(upon)	*legein*	(say, study of)
8. Aspect	*ad-*	(to, towards)	*specere*	(see)
9. Uncomplicated	*un-*	(not)	*plicare*	(fold)
	com-	(together, with)		
10. Nonextended	*non-*	(not)	*tendere*	(stretch)
	ex-	(out, beyond)		
11. Reproduction	*re-*	(back, again)	*ducere*	(lead)
	pro-	(forward, for)		
12. Indisposed	*in-*	(not)	*ponere*	(put, place)
	dis-	(apart, not)		
13. Oversufficient	*over-*	(above)	*facere*	(make, do)
	sub-	(under)		
14. Mistranscribe	*mis-*	(wrong)	*scribere*	(write)
	trans-	(across, beyond)		

The remainder of the text will give you the needed experience to use these shortcuts to full advantage.

Turn to the Appendix for some indication as to the number of words which can be dealt with more effectively through knowledge of only one prefix—in this case, the prefix *pre-*. Remember also that in every specialized field, such as medicine, law, or one of the sciences, there are additional technical terms not even listed in the dictionary which can be understood more clearly through attention to prefix and root elements. Note the listing of words taken from a medical dictionary. In this listing only those words not listed in the collegiate dictionary are included.

Getting maximum results

Read each frame carefully, several times if you are in doubt about the right answer. Remember, there are usually a number of clues in every frame which should guide you to the right answer.

To insure best progress, take the time you need to reason out the answer. Take this frame from the unit on *mono-*:

A one-legged creature is a _____pode.

It is easy to fill in the right answer (*mono-*) and hurry on to the next frame. If you do, however, you are not taking full advantage of observations that may well double the effectiveness of the text. A more thoughtful look at that frame should give you reason to suspect that *pode* means "leg"—"one-legged" equals *monopode*.

Put a check in the margin by such frames. When you finish the entire unit, check your assumptions with the dictionary, in this case by looking up *pode*. This will acquaint you with the Greek word *pous, podos*, meaning "foot." This in turn brings such words as *tripod, podium, pleopod, podagra, podiatrist,* and *podophyllin* into sharper focus. This is why you should reason your way carefully through even the most obvious frames to make certain you note all pertinent relationships.

Opportunities for review are also frequently introduced. Take full advantage of them. Note the following frame from the unit on *pro-*:

If *regress* means "to go back," and *egress,* "to go out," "to go forward" would be to make _____gress.

This single frame provides four opportunities: (1) to review the meaning of *re-*, (2) to preview the meaning of *e-*, (3) to reason out the meaning of *pro-*, and (4) to arrive at a meaning for *gress.*

As soon as you have written down your answer, check its correctness *immediately.* Research points up the importance of that immediate check.

Whenever you miss an item, go back over the preceding few frames to see what clues you apparently missed. Your ability to concentrate and think should show improvement along with increased word power—all three so essential to effective living in this print-filled world.

J. I. B.

St. Paul, Minnesota

Part I Diagnosis

Diagnosis

The first step in building a better vocabulary is to note carefully every new word you meet. For example, one student during his first week in college came across the following words. He discovered *ebracteate* and *exospore* in his Botany text. He heard a medical doctor use the word *exostosis* and a geologist refer to *extravasate*. From general reading he soon extended the list. How many of his words do you know without consulting the dictionary? Try the following test to see. Enter the answers in the column headed I.

		I	II
1. ebracteate (Botany)	1) with bracts 2) without bracts 3) rounded bracts 4) pointed bracts 5) flexible bracts	1____	1____
2. exospore (Botany)	1) core 2) source 3) middle layer 4) outer layer of a spore	2____	2____
3. extravasate (Geology)	1) melt 2) shrink 3) harden 4) crack 5) erupt	3____	3____
4. exostosis (Medicine)	1) outgrowth 2) leg bone 3) paralysis 4) joint 5) sore	4____	4____
5. ebullition	1) blackness 2) boiling out 3) seeping in 4) repair 5) warmth	5____	5____
6. elide	1) omit 2) slide 3) glisten 4) warm 5) soften	6____	6____
7. expunge	1) dive in 2) soak 3) erase 4) swim 5) save	7____	7____
8. effete	1) worn out 2) athletic 3) difficult 4) shut in 5) wealthy	8____	8____
9. exhume	1) moisten 2) work 3) put in 4) pay for 5) dig out	9____	9____
10. evulsion	1) hatred 2) poor opinion 3) lotion 4) rooting out 5) description	10____	10____

3

This text is structured to let you learn much through little. To illustrate, look back at the test you just completed. If you know and apply *one* single piece of information, you should improve your score by about 36%. At least that is what one group of 78 adults did, the greatest improvement being from one right the first time to nine the second, with no help from the dictionary.

When you know that all ten words in the test contain a form of the prefix *ex-*, meaning "out," you have a key to the meaning of over a thousand such words of desk dictionary size, plus hundreds more from the big unabridged dictionary. To explore the advantage of this approach, take the test again, entering your new scores in the column headed II. This time lean heavily on your shortcut; always select the choice closest to the meaning "out" in each case. Check both sets of answers when you have finished, using the key on page 252. The advantage in this approach should be obvious, both in arriving closer to word meaning as well as in remembering meanings.

Now that you know just what this approach can do, you should, as a next step, get an in-depth diagnostic picture of your present abilities in dealing with prefix and root elements. The following four-part test should provide that picture. Complete it without the help of a dictionary before reading further.

Name _____

Diagnostic Test

(Complete this four-part diagnostic test without using a dictionary)

Name _____

Test A

Information

1. *re-* means 1) together; 2) upon; 3) back or again; 4) behind; 5) out of   1. _____

2. *mono-* means 1) some; 2) now; 3) still; 4) alone; 5) almost   2. _____

3. *sub-* means 1) beside; 2) apart from; 3) out; 4) under; 5) in front of   3. _____

4. *mis-* means 1) wrong; 2) cruel; 3) different; 4) late; 5) old   4. _____

5. *com-* means 1) every; 2) through; 3) after; 4) together; 5) in   5. _____

6. *ad-* means 1) for; 2) with; 3) to or toward; 4) from; 5) only or without   6. _____

7. *inter-* means 1) inside; 2) between; 3) near; 4) forward; 5) among   7. _____

8. *ab-* means 1) bad; 2) take out; 3) below; 4) away from; 5) not   8. _____

9. *pro-* means 1) together with; 2) to go; 3) behind; 4) forward; 5) outside   9. _____

10. *para-* means 1) more; 2) beginning; 3) present; 4) past; 5) beside   10. _____

11. *scribere* means 1) write; 2) stretch; 3) speak; 4) scratch; 5) frighten   11. _____

12. *videre* means 1) eat; 2) catch; 3) value; 4) shake; 5) see   12. _____

13. *ferre* means 1) bear or carry; 2) float; 3) rust; 4) put or place; 5) enter   13. _____

14. *facere* means 1) put; 2) fear; 3) make; 4) fill; 5) lead   14. _____

15. *sequi* means 1) decorate; 2) quiet; 3) cure; 4) follow; 5) preach   15. _____

16. *logos* (legein) means 1) speech or science; 2) locate or find; 3) raise; 4) limit; 5) leave   16. _____

17. *vertere* means 1) turn; 2) speak; 3) inform; 4) watch; 5) voyage   17. _____

18. *mittere* means 1) send; 2) catch; 3) release; 4) tire; 5) earn   18. _____

19. *sedere* means 1) cut off; 2) speak; 3) sit; 4) select; 5) satisfy   19. _____

20. *claudre* means 1) climb; 2) divide; 3) clean; 4) eliminate;
     5) shut   20. _____

Name _____

Test B

Identification

1. *Correlation* contains a form of 1) *contra-;* 2) *circum-;* 3) *re-;*
   4) *ab-;* 5) none of the preceding prefixes   1. ____

2. *Monopoly* contains a form of 1) *homo-;* 2) *multi-;* 3) *mal-;*
   4) *mono-;* 5) none of the preceding prefixes   2. ____

3. *Suppress* contains a form of 1) *super-;* 2) *supra-;* 3) *pro-;*
   4) *sub;* 5) none of the preceding prefixes   3. ____

4. *Misnomer* contains a form of 1) *mal-;* 2) *mid-;* 3) *mega-;*
   4) *mis-;* 5) none of the preceding prefixes   4. ____

5. Collaborate contains a form of 1) *coma-;* 2) *counter-;* 3) *contra-*
   4) *cata;* 5) none of the preceding prefixes   5. ____

6. *Adder-* contains a form of 1) *ana-;* 2) *ad-;* 3) *amphi-;* 4) *de-;*
   5) none of the preceding prefixes   6. ____

7. *Intercept* contains a form of 1) *in-;* 2) *intro-;* 3) *ex-;* 4) *inter-;*
   5) none of the preceding prefixes   7. ____

8. *Aversion* contains a form of 1) *ab-;* 2) *apo-;* 3) *ana-;* 4) *ex-;*
   5) none of the preceding prefixes   8. ____

9. *Reproduce* contains a form of 1) *retro-;* 2) *pro-;* 3) *ob-;* 4) *post;*
   5) none of the preceding prefixes   9. ____

10. *Parallel* contains a form of 1) *pan-;* 2) *pyro-;* 3) *para-;* 4) *peri-;*
    5) none of the preceding prefixes   10. ____

11. The word *nondescript* contains a form of 1) *densus;* 2) *crescere;*
    3) *stringere;* 4) *ducere;* 5) none of the preceding roots   11. ____

12. *Video* contains a form of 1) *videre;* 2) *vincere;* 3) *volvere;*
    4) *verus;* 5) none of the preceding roots   12. ____

13. *Feature* contains a form of 1) *ferre;* 2) *forma;* 3) *fundere;*
    4) *fluere;* 5) none of the preceding roots   13. ____

14. *Factory* contains a form of 1) *actus;* 2) *facere;* 3) *capere;*
    4) *agere;* 5) none of the preceding roots   14. ____

15. *Sequel* contains a form of 1) *guaerere;* 2) *sequi;* 3) *scopein;* 4) *sentire;* 5) none of the preceding roots   15. ____

16. *Sociology* contains a form of 1) *senex;* 2) *logos;* 3) *ludere;* 4) *cito;* 5) none of the preceding roots   16. ____

17. *Versatile* contains a form of 1) *vertere;* 2) *sedere;* 3) *venire;* 4) *jacere;* 5) none of the preceding roots   17. ____

18. *Admission* contains a form of 1) *agere;* 2) *dicere;* 3) *mutare;* 4) *mittere;* 5) none of the preceding roots   18. ____

19. *Sediment* probably contains a form of 1) *sedere;* 2) *sentire;* 3) *dicere;* 4) *cedere;* 5) none of the preceding roots   19. ____

20. *Include* probably contains a form of 1) *caput;* 2) *clinare;* 3) *credere;* 4) *claudeie;* 5) none of the preceding roots   20. ____

Name _____

Test C

Application

1. *relumed* means 1) lighted again; 2) torn into bits; 3) filled up; 4) brightened; 5) lined up   1. _____

2. *monostich* means 1) headache; 2) catalog; 3) radio; 4) line of poetry; 5) lining   2. _____

3. *sublunary* means 1) luminous; 2) oval; 3) solar; 4) unreasoning; 5) earthy   3. _____

4. *miscreant* means 1) dramatist; 2) executive; 3) speaker; 4) heretic; 5) warrior   4. _____

5. *compendium* means 1) summary; 2) pencil; 3) pretense; 4) extension; 5) discarding   5. _____

6. *adminicular* means 1) retiring; 2) small; 3) broken down; 4) strange; 5) helping   6. _____

7. *interlope* means 1) elude; 2) chase; 3) intrude; 4) modify; 5) limp   7. _____

8. *aberrant* means 1) inclusive; 2) relevant; 3) tired; 4) abnormal; 5) sane   8. _____

9. *prolocutor* means 1) spouse; 2) spokesman; 3) orator; 4) plan; 5) typist   9. _____

10. *paradigm* means 1) falsehood; 2) model; 3) exception; 4) eruption; 5) problem   10. _____

11. *escritoire* means 1) writing desk; 2) raven; 3) drinking fountain; 4) paper; 5) bank   11. _____

12. *vis-à-vis* means 1) back to back; 2) new; 3) alike; 4) face to face; 5) side by side   12. _____

13. *feracious* means 1) fierce; 2) gentle; 3) solid; 4) barren; 5) fruitful   13. _____

14. *facile* means 1) skillful; 2) struggling; 3) conservative; 4) beginning; 5) deserving   14. _____

15. *sequela* means 1) remedy; 2) following thing; 3) quiz; 4) struggle; 5) big tree   15. _____

16. *logogriph* means 1) wooden peg; 2) gun; 3) container; 4) word puzzle; 5) handle   16. _____

17. *divert* means 1) remove; 2) turn aside; 3) make ready; 4) display; 5) remain   17. _____

18. *missive* means 1) nurse; 2) message; 3) star; 4) question; 5) designer   18. _____

19. *sedate* means 1) worldly; 2) composed; 3) religious; 4) secretive; 5) slovenly   19. _____

20. *claustral* means 1) fatty; 2) harmful; 3) confined; 4) clear; 5) stormy   20. _____

Name _____

Test D

Generalization

1. The prefix *dis-* is not in 1) *displease;* 2) *indifferent;* 3) *diffuse;*
   4) *distract;* 5) *dish*   1. _____

2. The prefix *de-* is not in 1) *defer;* 2) *debar;* 3) *condescend;*
   4) *decrease;* 5) *death*   2. _____

3. Which of the following prefixes is most likely to change in form?
   1) *hyper-;* 2) *pre-;* 3) *mono-;* 4) *com-;* 5) *de-*   3. _____

4. The prefix *ex-* is usually spelled *ef-* before a root beginning
   with 1) *f;* 2) *g;* 3) *s;* 4) *m;* 5) *c*   4. _____

5. If there were a prefix *rib-* to be combined with *port,* the probable
   form would be 1) *ripport;* 2) *ribport;* 3) *riport;* 4) *ribbort;*
   5) *ribort*   5. _____

6. The most frequent variations in prefix form are found with the
   prefixes ending in 1) a vowel; 2) a consonant; 3) a diphthong;
   4) a double vowel; 5) an *m*   6. _____

7. In English words, the *-ere* or *-are* of many Latin roots is normally 1) retained; 2) changed to *-er;* 3) changed to *-or;*
   4) changed to *-re;* 5) dropped   7. _____

8. If you combined the imaginary prefix *ud-* with *nex,* the probable
   resulting form would be 1) *unnex;* 2) *udnex;* 3) *uddex;*
   4) *unex;* 5) *udex*   8. _____

9. Variations in original classical root elements coming over into
   English usually occur in what part? 1) no particular part; 2) the
   last part; 3) the middle part; 4) the first part   9. _____

10. English words derived from classical sources make up about
    how much of our language? 1) 20%; 2) 30%; 3) 40%;
    4) 50%; 5) 60%   10. _____

11. The Latin word *fluo,* found in *fluid* and *flux,* probably means
    1) force; 2) year; 3) flow; 4) harden; 5) file   11. _____

12. *Omni-,* found in *omnibus, omnipresent,* and *omniverous,* probably means 1) solid; 2) free; 3) single; 4) old; 5) all

12. _____

13. *Fundo,* found in *funnel* and *refund,* probably means 1) shape; 2) bind; 3) pour; 4) pay; 5) fall

13. _____

14. *Ardeo,* found in *ardor* and *arson,* probably means 1) burn; 2) tree; 3) love; 4) cruel; 5) equal

14. _____

15. *Meta-,* found in *metamorphosis* and *metathesis,* probably means 1) fixed; 2) altered; 3) spoken; 4) outlined; 5) discovered

15. _____

16. *Valeo,* found in *valor,* and *invalid,* probably means 1) level; 2) weak; 3) old; 4) strong; 5) colorful

16. _____

17. *Dies,* found in *diary* and *diurnal,* probably means 1) book; 2) day; 3) pen; 4) year; 5) skill

17. _____

18. *Aristos,* found in *aristocrat,* probably means 1) best; 2) ancient; 3) vain; 4) recent; 5) artistic

18. _____

19. After thinking of some words beginning with *mega-,* which meaning seems best for that combination form? 1) limited; 2) sure; 3) middling; 4) powerful; 5) artificial

19. _____

20. After thinking of some words derived from *pendeo,* which meaning seems best? 1) hang; 2) judge; 3) pierce; 4) exchange; 5) feel

20. _____

Name _____

Report sheet for initial scores on Four-Part Diagnostic Test:

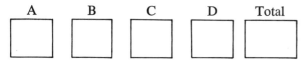

A   B   C   D   Total

Enter your scores in the corresponding boxes on the Profile Sheet, page 16.
Final scores on Four-Part Diagnostic Test:

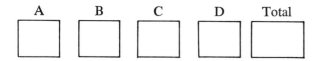

A   B   C   D   Total

Enter these scores on the Profile Sheet, page 16, using a dotted line instead of a solid line to connect the scores so that your progress may be more easily noted.

Self-interpreting profile

This vocabulary test provides you with a four-dimension picture of yourself. Enter your raw score for each part of the test in the appropriate box at the top of each column. Draw a heavy line through that number in the column below. Connect the heavy lines to make your profile.

To get your percentile rank, look along the line in which your raw score is located to the column at the left of the page. For example, if your score on Test A is 15, look at the percentile rank column opposite that number, which indicates the 84-86 percentile rank.

If your score in any of the columns is above the top dotted line, you are high in that area—among the top 25%. If any score is between the two dotted lines, you are about average—among the middle 50%. If any score is below the bottom dotted line, you are low in that area—among the bottom 25%.

Interpreting your profile

Study your profile carefully. It should indicate strengths or weaknesses which will let you direct your learning efforts to best advantage. What will it tell you about yourself? It will uncover the four important stages of knowing, leading to an in-depth awareness of language and to a group of key principles which will supply a specialized derivational context to supplement the all-important general context.

The word *know,* even in an abridged dictionary, has over ten different meanings. In one sense, to *know* the twenty prefix and fourteen root elements covered in this text—the most useful vocabulary-building short cuts in the English language—would require only a few minutes of learning time. You could sit down right now and memorize them all in a matter of minutes.

If your score on Part A of the test was below average—11 or less—you know that your rote knowledge of prefix and root elements is below average. To expedite learning, pinpoint which elements you know by trying the following test that summarizes the material offered in the text.

%-ile	A	B	C	D	Total
99	20	19	18-20	19	65+
96-98	19	17-18	16-17	18	63-64
93-95	17-18	16		17	60-62
90-92	16	15	15	16	59
87-89			14	15	57-58
84-86	15	14			55-56
81-83					54
78-80	14		13		53
75-77	– – – – – – – – – – – – – – – – – – –			14 – – – – –	52 – –
72-74		13			51
69-71	13		12		50
66-68					48-49
63-65				13	
60-62			11		47
57-59	12			12	46
54-56		12			45
51-53					
48-50	————————————————		10 ———		44 —
45-47	11			11	43
42-44					40-42
39-41		11			
36-38	10			10	39
33-35			9		
30-32		10			38
27-29				9	37
24-26	– – – – 9 – – – – – – – – – – –		8 – – – – – – – – – – –		36 – –
21-23		9			
18-20			7	8	35
15-17	8	8			34
12-14					33
9-11	7	7	6	7	31-32
6-8		6	5		27-30
3-5	6	4-5	4	5-6	22-26
0-2	5	0-3	0-3	0-4	14-21

The twenty prefixes

Enter the proper meaning for each of the following prefixes.

1. *pre-* means _____   11. *non-* means _____

2. *de-* means _____   12. *ex-* means _____

3. *inter-* means _____   13. *re-* means _____

4. *ob-* means _____   14. *pro-* means _____

5. *in-* means _____   15. *in-* means _____

6. *mono-* means _____   16. *dis-* means _____

7. *epi-* means _____   17. *over-* means _____

8. *ad-* means _____   18. *sub-* means _____

9. *un-* means _____   19. *mis-* means _____

10. *com-* means _____   20. *trans-* means _____

The fourteen roots

Enter the proper meaning for each of the following roots.

1. *capere* means _____   8. *specere* means _____

2. *tenere* means _____   9. *plicare* means _____

3. *mittere* means _____ 10. *tendere* means _____

4. *ferre* means _____   11. *ducere* means _____

5. *stare* means _____   12. *ponere* means _____

6. *graphein* means _____ 13. *facere* means _____

7. *logos* means _____   14. *scribere* means _____

Check with the answers on page 252.

But rote knowledge of prefix and root meanings, important though that information is, is but a beginning. Still another dictionary definition of *know* is "to be able to distinguish; recognize"—quite different from fixing something securely in the mind or memory.

Now look at your score on the second test, Test B, which measures your present skill in identifying these elements in their natural habitat—words. Obviously if you have more than usual difficulty identifying the presence of a prefix or root in a word, knowledge of its meaning has little or no value. Similarly, if you are better than average at identifying such elements but do not know what they mean, your vocabulary-building efforts will also suffer.

The complexity of identification can be further demonstrated by asking you to look over the following twelve words, checking any that contain the prefix *ad-*.

1. abbreviate _____	7. accumulate _____
2. attract _____	8. arrive _____
3. associate _____	9. allude _____
4. annex _____	10. agglutinate _____
5. ascend _____	11. append _____
6. afferent _____	12. adynamic _____

You should have checked every single word except for the last one, which begins with an *ad-*. As you can see, accurate identification demands a special kind of insight. Your score on Test B indicates how much of that know-how is already yours. To spot *ad-* in *admit* is relatively easy. Put another prefix in front of it, as with the word in*ad*vertant, and *ad-* may pass unnoticed. In *adynamic* the combining form *dyn-* or *dyna-,* meaning "power," may go unnoticed, the *d* joined mentally with the *a* instead of with the *yn,* where it belongs. The words *typical* and *atypical* provide helpful insight into the *dynamic/adynamic* forms, keeping the *a* and *d* separate.

Now look at your score on Test C. How much skill do you presently have in arriving at or closer to word meanings through applying your knowledge of word elements? After all, knowing and identifying a tool as a soldering iron does not necessarily mean you can use it skillfully. Similarly, you can score at the eightieth percentile in the first two tests and down at the thirtieth on Test C.

The items for this part of the test were specially constructed to provide the best possible measure of the pay-off step for this approach to vocabulary. Toward that end, words were chosen from the Thorndike and Lorge research that occurred rarely in English, most of them no more than once in a million words. All twenty contained a prefix or root element from Test A and for identification in Test B. Thus if you 1) identified the element properly and 2) knew what it meant, you would be led to the meaning of the word in question.

To indicate the structural pattern used, take this example:

accolade means 1) change, 2) remedy, 3) mystery, 4) award, 5) refrain.

If you know that *accolade* contains a form of the prefix *ad-* and know, further, that *ad-* means "to or toward," apply that knowledge to arrive at word meaning. Ask yourself which of the five choices is closest to the concept of action "to or toward." *Change* can be "to" or "away." With *remedy,* "for" seems closer than "to." The most natural connection with *mystery* is "about." An *award* is something given "to" someone—a move "toward" recognizing some service or ability. "From" is the concept usually paired with *refrain.*

In short, when you apply your knowledge of word elements properly in this way, you should 1) arrive at the meaning of *accolade* and 2) remember that meaning more easily.

With far too much of our learning we stop with the application step—the pay-off step. When we do, however, we overlook the one step that will facilitate our handling of the thousands of prefix and root elements never once mentioned in these pages. The procedure is generalization. We must begin to look at one specific prefix or root, not as one thing but as a possible prototype or archetype for all prefix and root elements. Only then can these few elements contribute most to our understanding of all other such elements.

Your score on Test D suggests how well you make accurate generalizations about other relatively rare or even made-up elements. A low score here suggests the need for a change of attitude—one that will bring you the in-depth insights of most value to you in dealing with word elements. This last test focuses on still another meaning of *know*—the ability to draw accurate inferences or meaningful conclusions about general behavior from a few specific instances.

By some, rote memory is considered the greatest waste in education. The forgetting curve in a typical psychology text is a dramatic reminder of how quickly we forget. That is why it is so important, as in this text, to involve, through a programmed format focused on four kinds of steps, important problem-solving relationships and the higher mental processes. Learning so structured is relatively permanent.

Now you know where to put most emphasis as you work through the remainder of this book, thanks to the insights derived from your profile sheet.

Part II Prefixes

1   *Mnemonics* ∿

How should you work through this new kind of book
to insure best results?

First, you must properly manage the mechanics of
using this program. Otherwise it will be no more effective than an ordinary text.

Try the first frame.

    Read the entire frame.

    Write in the required response.

    Check the answers, located in the right hand column,
    a line lower than the question.

Do not look at the answers before you have read the
entire frame and written in the required response.

1. If *mnemonics* is a word derived from the Greek word
mnasthai, meaning "to remember," you would expect
it to mean "the art or science of improving one's
_____ory."

When you have made your response, check its accuracy
by turning to the outside column, examining the answer.

                Here is the answer: *mem*ory

Whenever your answer is wrong, reread the frame to see what clues you overlooked. Put a heavy X in the margin beside any item missed. For example, in the first frame the similarity between *mnem*onics and re*mem*ber should have suggested *mem*ory. When your answer is right, go on to the next frame.

2. One important way of aiding memory is by associating what is to be learned—what is, in that sense, unknown —with what is already learned or _____.

Again, context should help you to a correct response. Notice how this context suggests the fairly common analogy-type test item, frequently used in graduate school admission tests. Here is a sample: *street* is to *horizontal* as *building* is to _____. Of the choices—*high, brick,* and *vertical*—of course the last one is correct. In the frame you just read, the *to-be-learned* is to the *unknown* as the *already-learned* is to

known

_____. Most frames, just as this one, contain hints intended to sharpen your awareness of contextual clues.

Check your response in the outside column before starting the third frame.

It has been said that any subject with a logical structure can be taught in half the time with half the effort through a program. Remember to give each frame thoughtful consideration *before* looking at the answer. Otherwise you make this a conventional textbook and lose the learning advantage of the programmed form.

3. In learning prefix and root elements, therefore, think in terms of establishing meaningful a_____ between the known and the unknown.

When you have completed the frame, check your response in the outside column.

associations

Actually, the key word *associating,* in the second frame,
was your strongest cue. This link back to a preceding
frame was made to remind you to do each item in its
proper turn and, when in difficulty, to think back or
look back to the preceding frame for additional help.

In addition to proper management of the machinery,
be sure to take full advantage of all underlying principles and techniques mentioned. The first two frames,
for example, introduced the concept of mnemonics,
giving you a definition and understanding of its meaning. The third frame, however, attempted to get you
to think beyond a specific response to a general rule or
principle, useful not only with the thirty-four elements
to be studied in depth in this text, but with hundreds
of others not mentioned here. In short, remember that
mnemonics has a wide, not limited, application.

In learning anything, a major problem lies in moving
from theory to practice, from verbal know-how to
operational know-how, from knowing to applying.
Knowing what a gun is does not mean you are auto-
matically an expert marksman. Similarly, knowing
what mnemonics is does not of itself mean you apply
that principle effectively.

The next frame is typical of those used in this text to
expedite your progress from knowing to applying. In
it you will be led to apply mnemonics as an aid in remembering one meaning of *de-.* Try it.

4. For example, to remember that *de-* means "down," associate it with the word *depress*. When you depress a key on a typewriter, you literally press it ＿＿＿＿＿.

down

The fifth frame provides for a review and reinforcing of prefix meaning. Do not be disturbed over the ease with which most frames can be completed. In mastering almost any subject matter, one usually picks up some misconceptions and half-truths along with the truth. Once a misconception takes root and becomes established, the learning process is greatly complicated. This explains in part an advantage of the programmed approach; with a programmed format, if a wrong answer is made, it is immediately corrected before it has a chance to take root.

5. And when you descend a ladder, you come ＿＿＿＿＿ it.

down

The next frame introduces you to a technique, not for remembering but for discovering meanings—a way of reasoning about words so as to arrive at prefix or root meanings. When you have developed sureness with this approach and made it habitual, you have a most useful word attack technique at your command.

Whenever you see a strange prefix or root, your first move should be to think of a word or two containing the element, in hopes of seeing a common meaning. For example, if you wonder what *mega-* means, you might think of *megaphone* or *megaton* bomb. From these examples you should be able to come fairly close to the dictionary meaning of *mega-* "large, great, powerful."

6. This thought pattern, in reverse, will often lead you to prefix meanings. For example, another common meaning of *de-* is found in the word *depart,* which does not mean to go down but to go _____ from one place to another.

away

Here is another review frame, to fix the two common meanings of *de-* more firmly in mind. This is part of the desirable reinforcing which you will find from time to time in this text.

7. Here the words *depress* and *depart* serve as mnemonic aids to help you remember that *de-* commonly means "_____" or "_____."

down
away

The next nine frames cover prefix elements not included among the thirty-four to be studied in depth. They are designed to set the pattern for you to use with any elements to be learned. Go right ahead.

8. To remember that *homo-* means "same," associate it with _____ milk—milk which is the same throughout, not separating into cream.

homogenized

9. To remember that *hydro-* means "water," think of a fire engine standing by a red fire _____ to which the hose is connected.

hydrant

10. To remember that *hypo-* means "under," think of where the doctor puts the _____ needle when he gives you a shot in the arm.

hypodermic

11. To remember that *hyper-* means "over" or "beyond," think of someone who is sensitive far beyond the super-sensitive—someone who is _____.

hypersensitive

12. To remember that *syn-* means "with or together," think of *synthesis,* the putting _____ of parts of elements so as to make a whole.

together

13. To remember that *dia-* means "through" or "across," visualize a circle and the line passing directly through the center: this line we call the _____.

diameter

14. To remember that *para-* means "beside," visualize two _____ lines, lines which run side by side without meeting.

parallel

15. To remember that *per-* means "through" think of brewing coffee in a _____ in which boiling water bubbles up through a tube.

percolator

16. To remember that *ab-* means "away," think of being away from class or _____.

absent

In the preceding frames, the prefix meaning was always given, the problem being to arrive at an appropriate word to serve as a mnemonic. In the following frame, you must note similarities and draw inferences based on both prefix and root elements. Frames of this kind are intended to establish more effective thought patterns for analyzing and understanding words.

17. If a hexagon is a six-sided figure and a polygon is a many-sided figure, *poly-* probably means "_____."

many

The opposite of word analysis is word building. In the next frame you are given a definition and a known part. Problem? To build a word to fit the definition! If you run into difficulties, always remember to look back at the preceding frame.

18. If *glot* comes from the Greek word *glotta,* meaning "tongue," a person who speaks many languages or tongues would rightly be called a p_____.

p*olyglot*

In the next three frames, you face a more difficult task. You must arrive at prefix meaning through skillful use of context and word meaning.

19. If in a submarine a periscope lets you look around, you would infer that *peri-* probably means "a_____."

a*round*

20. If a microscope is an instrument for looking at small objects, and a telescope, for looking at far objects, *tele-* probably means "_____."

far

21. If an archetype is the first or original type, *archi-* probably means "_____" or "_____."

first
original

Since the remaining frames are similar in pattern to some already completed, you need no further guidance.

22. When you want to remember that *ante-* means "before," think of your ancestors or _____cedents —those who came before you.

*ante*cedents

23. *Anti-,* on the other hand, means "against," as in the type of gun used against aircraft, called _____.

antiaircraft

24. The meaning of *en-* is easily remembered if you think that *enclose* and the less common *inclose* both mean "to close _____."

in

25. If a tricycle has three wheels, you can easily infer, from *bicycle,* that the prefix *bi-* means "_____."

two

26. To remember that *mal-* means "bad" or "badly," think of the word which means "badly adjusted," as in the sentence, "He is socially _____."

maladjusted

Now that you have completed Unit I, *Mnemonics,* you can see more clearly how to work through the following units. You should be alert to the presence of basic principles. In this unit the basic principle is:

Review frame

In memorizing prefix and root elements, use *mne-mnics,* or associations, as learning aids.

You can also see what steps were taken to help you develop real skill in applying this principle of learning.

Review

Since most of the prefixes and combining forms mentioned in Unit I were given only scant attention, review them from time to time, using the following table. Cover the two right-hand columns until you have mentally supplied the answers. Then go to the next item to check accuracy.

PREFIX	SUGGESTED MNEMONIC	COMMON MEANING
1. *homo-*	homogenized	"same"
2. *hydro-*	hydrant	"water"
3. *hypo-*	hypodermic	"under"
4. *hyper-*	hypersensitive	"over" or "beyond"
5. *dia-*	diameter	"through"
6. *para-*	parallel	"beside"
7. *per-*	percolator	"through"
8. *ab-*	absent	"away"
9. *poly-*	polygon	"many"
10. *peri-*	periscope	"around"
11. *tele-*	telescope	"far"
12. *archi-*	archetype	"first" or "original"
13. *ante-*	antecedents	"before"
14. *anti-*	antiaircraft	"against"
15. *en-*	enclose	"in"
16. *bi-*	bicycle	"two"
17. *mal-*	maladjusted	"bad" or "badly"
18. *glot*	polyglot	"tongue"

2   *Pre* ∾

Since *pre-* is the first of the prefixes to be studied in depth, additional guidance will be provided with some of the frames to insure maximum benefits from this and all following units.

The first frame suggests a way of determining the meaning of any prefix as well as leading directly to the meaning of *pre-*.

1. If *preview* means "to view before" and *preheat,* "to heat before," you would assume *pre-* means "_____."

before

2. But *before* has several shades of meaning. In which one of the following words, for example, does *pre-* have the meaning "before in place, front, anterior"?

    prescribe
    prewar
    prefix

prefix

33

3. In which one of the following words does *pre-* mean "before in time, previously"?

> prefer
> prearrange
> pretend

prearrange

4. In which one of the following words does *pre-* mean "before others in rank or degree"?

> preeminent
> precancel
> preliminary

preeminent

Knowing prefix meaning or shades of meaning, however, is only a start. The next problem is identifying the prefix in its normal setting—a word. The next four frames will help you discover one important rule-of-thumb check—a principle you can begin to use immediately with all prefixes.

5. Which of the following words are *still* words when you take off the *pre-*?

> precast
> pretzel
> preschool
> press

precast
preschool

6. Which two words would you infer do *not* contain the prefix *pre-*?

> precast
> pretzel
> preschool
> press

pretzel
press

Apparently the prefix *pre-* is found in most but not all words beginning with the letters *p, r, e.*

7. If *preschool* and *precast* both contain the prefix *pre-,* apparently one way to check the presence of a prefix is to determine if what follows the supposed prefix is a _____.

word

Apply this newly learned rule, and you can speed your move from theory right into practice.

8. With that rule of thumb in mind, which of the following words probably contains the prefix *pre-?*

    preternatural
    prester
    prenomınate
    preach

prenominate

Of course, two checks will serve better than one, especially if neither covers all situations. The following frames give you a second rule of thumb.

9. In which of the following words can you substitute another prefix, such as *in-,* for the prefix *pre-?*

    preclude
    predator

preclude

10. Which of the following words probably contains the prefix *pre-?*

    preclude
    predator
    pressure

preclude

11. Now you have an additional rule-of-thumb check on the presence of a prefix. See if another _____ can be substituted in its place.

prefix

12. Taking off the *pre-* in *preclude* does not leave a word, *but* substituting another _____ for *pre-* will make a different word.

prefix

Remember to try both rule-of-thumb checks. If either one or both work, you have reason to suspect the presence of a prefix.

It is not enough to know prefix meanings and be able to identify their presence in words. What might be called the *"pay-off"* step is still to be taken—the useful application of this knowledge in dealing both with familiar and strange words.

With this knowledge you can make generalizations which will apply with equal pertinence to the *thousands* of prefixes not specifically dealt with here.

In the following frames you can put your prefix knowledge to work in a variety of common situations.

13. Prefix knowledge makes familiar words more interesting. Take *prelude*. The prefix reminds us that a prelude is something played _____ the main performance begins.

before

14. If *post-* means "after," as in *postscript* or *postpone,* something played after the main performance would be appropriately called, not a prelude, but a _____.

postlude

15. And strange words become less so with prefix knowledge to apply. If you hear that someone has a predilection for jazz, the prefix suggests he puts it _____ other kinds of music.

before

16. In bridge, a preemptive bid is designed to get you the bid _____ your opponents have a chance to communicate information about their hands.

before

17. Your knowledge of *pre-* can help you define a *prelate* as a
 layman
 high-ranking clergyman
 church member.

high-ranking
clergyman
(before others
in rank)

18. And a prefect is probably

 a newspaper reporter
 an administrative official
 a policeman.

an administrative
official

Selecting the appropriate word to fit a given context or meaning is another facet of word power. Most of the remaining frames attempt to relate appropriateness of expression with words containing the prefix *pre-*.

19. We speak of the "before" part of a constitution as the _____ of the constitution.

*pre*amble

20. In this country, the man "before" all others in our national government is called the _____.

president

21. The "before" part of a book—usually found even before the introduction—is called the _____.

preface

22. If you premonish someone, you would infer you
    advise him
    help him
    forewarn him.

forewarn him

23. *Pre-* comes from the Latin *prae,* meaning "before." In ancient Rome, a man had three names. His prae-nomen would be his
    first name
    second name
    last name.

first name

24. To make ready beforehand for a situation is to _____ for it.

prepare

25. If someone judges a matter before he has sufficient evidence or knowledge, he is spoken of as a _____ individual.

prejudiced

This unit, like most of those which follow, is intended to teach four things: (1) what *pre-* means commonly and how to distinguish important shades of meaning, (2) how to identify the presence of *pre-* through use of two principles applicable to prefixes in general as well as to *pre-,* (3) how to apply prefix knowledge to make familiar words more interesting and strange words more understandable and rememberable, (4) how to select appropriate words for a given concept and develop added fluency with such words.

Now that you know exactly how to work through this new type of book to best advantage and what kinds of frames are used and why, the remaining units will all be in regular programed form, without interspersed comments.

Review statement

Remember the two rule-of-thumb checks for a possible prefix:

1) See if taking off the supposed prefix leaves a word.
2) See if you can substitute another prefix in its place to make a word.

To remember that *pre-* means "before," what word would you choose as a mnenomic aid? _____

You need not rely on premonitions or presentiments in building a vocabulary. Just start applying your prefix knowledge in dealing with strange or new words, such as the following.

1. _____

1. If you decide to *prelect,* you'll need to A) join a church, B) get before an audience, C) become a policeman, D) be nominated.

2. *precursor*—A) blasphemer, B) minister, C) helper, D) forerunner.

2. _____

3. *precocious*—A) slow-starting, B) before average, C) new, D) worn.

3. _____

4. *prefect*—A) sworn statement, B) student, C) chief official, D) soldier.

4. _____

5. *predilection*—A) abbreviation, B) gift, C) token, D) preference.

5. _____

Keep the prefix meaning in mind. To *prelect* is to lecture "before" a group. A *precursor* is one or that which goes "before" something. A *precocious* child is one which has matured "before" the average. A *prefect* is an official "before" others in rank. And if you have a *predilection* for something, you favor it "before" other things.

3 De ∿

1. Some prefixes, such as *pre-,* have only one common meaning. Others, such as *de-,* have several. You would infer from the words *descend* and *depress* that one meaning of *de-* is "_____," the opposite of "up."

down

2. That is why, when you look "down" on someone with disfavor or contempt, you may be said to ____spise him.

*de*spise

3. You should be able to arrive at another common meaning of *de-* through the word *depart.* Depart does not mean "to go down," as much as it does "to go a_____."

a*way*

4. Here is another example with this meaning of *de-.* When you take "away" the trailer that is attached to your car, you are said to _____ it.

detach

41

5. Still a third common meaning of *de-* is that of "reversing, undoing, or freeing from." In which of the following words is that meaning dominant?

   > defrost
   > detail
   > detect

defrost

6. Here is still another example of that meaning. Usually before a coded message can be understood, someone must de_____ it.

de*code*

7. Or take gas which is compressed into a small cylinder. When you release or free it, you _____compress it.

*de*compress

8. Finally, *de-* is sometimes used as an intensive, to catch the idea of "entirely or completely," as in *denude*— to make entirely or _____ nude.

completely

9. If a soldier deserts his post, which meaning of *de-* is uppermost?

   > entirely
   > reverse
   > down or away

down or away

10. If you are strongly inclined to turn "down" an invitation, you will probably de_____ to go.

de*cline*

11. Some foreigners found guilty of a crime are not imprisoned but taken to the nearest port and de_____ to their native land.

de*ported*

12. To get the reverse of *accelerate* (or speed up) just change the prefix. To slow down is to _____.

decelerate

13. Put your prefix knowledge to use with *detruncate*. You would expect it to mean

    to cut down
    to draw up
    to fill in
    to grow big.

to cut down

14. In a military operation, when you deploy your men you probably

    feed them
    draft them
    spread them out.

spread them out (or away)

15. With all the meanings in mind—down or away, reverse, entirely—you would assume *devolve* would mean

    to consider
    to pass
    to remain.

to pass

16. When a train jumps "away" from the rails, we say it is _____.

derailed

17. When you are forced to leave the highway because of road repairs, you turn "away" on a _____.

detour

18. Remembering that prefixes are often added to existing words to make new words, which one of the following words probably contains the prefix *de-?*

     deuce
     deform
     dental

deform

19. Remembering that other prefixes can usually be substituted in words containing a prefix, which one of the following words probably does *not* contain the prefix *de-?*

     demon
     deform
     defer

demon

20. Someone sent "away" to a convention as a representative is spoken of as a de_____.

de*legate*

21. If you delete a word from a letter, you take it a_____.

a*way*

22. The reverse of *inflate* is _____.

deflate

23. A shortage or deficit is also spoken of as a _____iency.

de*fic*iency

24. The reverse of *increase* is _____.

decrease

25. In conducting business affairs, remember that on income tax returns certain amounts can be taken "away" or de_____.

deducted

26. Word from abroad suggested that things were rapidly going "down" from bad to worse. In short, they were _____ing.

deteriorating

Review statement

To remember the four common meanings of *de-,* what words would make the best mnemonics?

1) For the meaning "down," the word de_____.

2) For the meaning "away," the word de_____.

3) For the meaning "to reverse or undo," the word de_____.

4) For use as an intensive, meaning "entirely or completely," the word de_____.

As further review, look at the words *defenestration, desuetude, defalcate, demise,* and *defray*—words which appear only about once in a million words, according to Thorndike's research. If you know even one, your vocabulary would be exceptionally good.

See how well you can apply prefix meaning to arrive at word meaning on the following difficult test:

1. _____

1. "You say he died from *defenestration?* Too bad! He shouldn't have A) eaten so much, B) lifted such a heavy load, C) driven so fast, D) thrown himself down from the 10th-story window."

2. _____

2. *desuetude*—A) smoothness, B) disuse, C) maturity, D) sun.

3. _____

3. *defalcate*—A) deafen, B) earn, C) embezzle, D) acquire.

4. _____

4. *demise*—A) opening, B) death, C) demon, D) rule.

5. _____

5. *defray*—A) pay, B) collect, C) budget, D) itemize.

4 *Mono* ∽

1. The Greek word *monos* means "one, single, or alone."
   If *lithos* means "stone," then a single stone shaped
   into a statue or monument would appropriately be
   called a _____lith.

   *mono*lith

2. If a democracy is government by the people, government by one person is rightly named a _____cracy.

   *mono*cracy

3. If marriage to many is polygamy, marriage to one
   would be _____.

   monogamy

4. How many colors would you expect to see in a monochrome? _____.

   one

5. How many limbs are paralyzed in a monoplegia case?
_____

one

6. The prefix *mono-* has two forms. It usually drops the final *o* before roots beginning with a vowel. For example, if *mono-* is added to *axial,* a root beginning with a vowel, the resulting combination should be spelled _____.

monaxial

7. The single or sole ruler of a state—sometimes called king or emperor—may also be called a _____arch.

*mon*arch

8. In biology, the term *monad* is used to describe any organism that consists of only _____ cell.

one

9. When someone becomes a monk and retires from the world because of religious vows, his place of residence is called a _____astery.

*mon*astery

10. If the Greek word *anthos* means "flower," the botanical term for a plant having only one flower would be _____anthous.

*mon*anthous

11. Keeping the two forms, *mono-* and *mon-,* in mind and remembering the final *o* is dropped before a root beginning with a vowel, determine which one of the following words probably contains the prefix *mono-*.

    montage
    monstrous
    mongrel
    monocarp

monocarp

12. The Latin word *oculus* means "eye." An eyeglass for one eye, formerly worn by Englishmen, is appropriately called a _____.

monocle

13. Words of one syllable are called _____syllabic words.

*mono*syllabic

14. As opposed to the polygenesis theory of the origin of life, there is the belief that all life descended from a "single" original organism. It is called the _____ theory.

monogenesis

15. In business, the exclusive control of a commodity or service is called a _____.

monopoly

16. If a *phobia* is an abnormal fear, an abnormal fear of being alone is appropriately called a _____.

monophobia

17. The Greek noun *pous, podos,* means "foot." In the word *monopode, mono-* is the prefix, and *pode,* the base or r_____t to which prefix and suffix elements are added.

root

18. In the word *podophyllin, pod* is in the position of and used as a _____, not a root.

prefix

19. A one-legged creature is a _____pode.

*mono*pode

20. The dictionary classifies word parts as prefix, root, suffix, or combining form. With *pous, podos,* used in both a prefix and root position, you would expect it to be classified, not as a prefix or root, but as a _____.

combining form

21. The Greek word *mania* means "madness." A craze or mania for some one thing is a _____.

monomania

22. How many actors would you expect to see in a mono-drama? _____.

one

23. If life seems to continue along in "one" way, with scarcely any variation, we call it mono_____.

mono*tonous*

24. If *gram* is a combining form meaning "something written," as in *telegram,* you would call a "single" figure or design made up of two or more letters a _____.

monogram

25. The presence in the blood of an abnormal number of leucocytes having only *one* nucleus is a condition called _____osis.

*mononucle*osis

Review statement

To remember that *mono-* means "one," what word will make a good mnenomic for you? _____

Remember that if an element such as *phono* is found in *phono*graph as well as tele*phone,* it is not a prefix or root but a combining form.

5   *Inter* ∽

1. *Inter-* comes from the Latin word *inter,* meaning "between or among." Action "between" two things would therefore properly be called an _____action.

   *inter*action

2. When *pre-* is added to *empt* to make *preempt,* both *e*'s are retained. In the same way, when you add *inter-* to *racial,* should you write it *interacial* or *interracial?* _____.

   interracial

3. If a *prelude* is something "played before" a performance, and *postlude,* something "played after" a performance, something "played between" acts should be called an _____.

   interlude

4. With *inter-,* one problem is to distinguish between *inter-,* and the prefix *in-* added to a word beginning with *ter.* In which of the following can you make a new word by substituting another prefix, such as *ex-,* for the five-letter prefix *inter-?*

   interpose
   internal

   interpose
   (expose)

51

5. In which of the words can you substitute another prefix for *in-*?

> interpose
> internal

> _____.

internal
(external)

6. Take the word *interminable*. Suppose you can think of no prefix to substitute for either *in-* or *inter-* to make a word. Try a suffix substitution. Substitute *-ate* for *-able*. Does *terminate* or *minate* seem a proper word?

> _____.

terminate

7. This rule-of-thumb check is a reminder that both prefixes and _____ are added to roots to make words.

suffixes

8. The Latin word *terminus* means "limit, boundary, or end." Drop the *-us* ending to get the common root form, *termin*. When you bring something to an "end" or conclusion, you termin_____ it.

termin*ate*

9. One who acts is an actor. In like manner, one who or that which terminates something is a _____.

terminator

10. The "end" of a railroad line or air line is spoken of as a terminus or termin_____.

termin*al*

11. Sometimes a root such as *termin* is shortened even farther. Part of *termin* names the stipulated length for holding an office, that is the _____ of office.

term

12. A few suffixes may even be added to this shortened form. For example, a limitless or boundless term of office could be called term_____.

term*less*

13. Word-analysis insights will develop rapidly as you manipulate these prefix, root, and _____ elements in this way.

suffix

14. And word parts help you define and remember words more easily. *Interim,* for example, probably means that period of time

    before
    between
    after.

between

15. The period of time "between" two events is called the time _____val.

*inter*val

16. If *erupt* means literally "to break out," and *disrupt,* "to break apart," what word means "to break between," as in conversation? _____.

interrupt

17. If things are scattered here and there "among" other things, they are _____spersed.

*inter*spersed

18. The region "between" planets is the _____-_____ary region.

*interplanet*ary

19. The time "between" acts or parts of a play or concert is called the _____.

intermission

20. In anatomy or zoology, the part "between" two nodes is called the _____.

internode

21. One who tries to hinder or prevent the delivery of the message wants to _____cept it.

*inter*cept

22. When you go to the leader of a labor union to plead for one of the members, you can be said to _____cede for him.

*inter*cede

23. An agreement between or among nations is spoken of as an _____ agreement.

international

24. When you interpolate something in a manuscript you probably

   insert new words
   rephrase
   condense
   study it.

insert new words

25. An interlocutor would be one who

   converses
   studies
   drives
   stands.

converses

26. Someone acting as mediator between two parties would be an _____ or intermediary.

intermediator

Review statement

27. One last reminder—*inter*- commonly means "b_____ or a_____."

b*etween* or a*mong*

Review Exercise I

A. In the blank after the prefix in the left-hand column, write the number, from the right-hand list, of the common meaning of the prefix. The same meaning may apply to more than one prefix. Some meanings will not be used at all.

1. *pre-* _____
2. *de-* _____
3. *mono-* _____
4. *inter-* _____
5. *ab-* or *abs-* _____

1. beside
2. between, among
3. out, outside
4. through
5. away, down
6. away
7. before
8. alone, one

B. In each of the following sets of words, there is one word which does *not* contain the prefix found in the rest of the words in that set. Using the principles covered in Unit 2, find that word and enter the appropriate letter in the blank at the right.

1. a) *pretzel,* b) *pretext,* c) *prefer,* d) *prebake*   1. _____
2. a) *deserve,* b) *detain,* c) *desist,* d) *derrick*   2. _____
3. a) *monorail,* b) *monaxial,* c) *mongrel,* d) *monologue*   3. _____
4. a) *intercede,* b) *intern,* c) *interweave,* d) *interlude*   4. _____
5. a) *abeam,* b) *abnormal,* c) *abrupt,* d) *abject*   5. _____

C. Use your knowledge of prefixes to help you deal with the relatively strange words in the following vocabulary test. Enter the appropriate letter in the blank at the right.

1. *prevision* means a) instruction, b) foresight, c) special showing, d) beauty   1. _____
2. *deterge* means to a) fill, b) start, c) raise, d) cleanse   2. _____
3. *monopode* means a) derailed, b) one-footed, c) magnified, d) crossbones   3. _____
4. *interpolate* means a) lengthen, b) check up, c) arouse, d) insert between   4. _____
5. *aberration* means a) deviation from norm, b) assistance, c) registration, d) correction of text   5. _____

(*Answers on page 253*)

Vocabulary Review List

Pre-
preview
preheat
prefix
prearrange
preeminent
precast
preschool
prenominate
preclude
prelude
predilection
preemptive
prelate
prefect
preamble
president
preface
premonish
praenomen
prepare
prejudiced

De-
descend
depress
despise
depart
detach
defrost
decode
decompress

denude
desert
decline
deport
decelerate
detruncate
deploy
devolve
derail
detour
deform
delegate
delete
deflate
deficit
deficiency
decrease
deduct
deteriorate

Mono-
monolith
monocracy
monogamy
monochrome
monoplegia
monaxial
monarch
monad
monastery
monanthous
monocarp

monocle
monosyllabic
monogenesis
monopoly
monophobia
monopode
monomania
monodrama
monotonous
monogram

Inter-
interaction
interracial
interlude
interpose
interim
interval
interrupt
intersperse
interplanetary
intermission
internode
intercept
intercede
international
interpolate
interlocutor
intermediator
intermediary

6 *Un* ~

1. The prefix *un-* has several different meanings. If we are uncomfortable we are not comfortable. If a box is untouched it is _____ touched.

not

2. In many words we can, without changing the meaning, substitute the word *not* for the negative prefix _____.

un-

3. If you are uncertain, you are _____certain.

not

4. But what about *untie?* Is this a simple negative? Or a reversal of verb action?

a reversal of verb action

5. In which of the following words is *un-* used to mean a reversal of verb action?

unaware
unfasten
unclean

unfasten

57

6. In a few rare but interesting words, *un-* has the force of an intensive. In which of these words is the verb action intensified (not reversed)?

unloosed
unchained
unrolled

unloosed
(same as *loosed*)

7. In which of the following words does *un-* have the force of a simple negative?

unbraid
unbroken
unburden

unbroken

8. When adding *un-* to a word or root beginning with *n*, as in *noted*, both *n*'s must be retained, giving us the correct spelling _____.

unnoted

9. If rules are "not" necessary, they are, in a word, _____.

unnecessary

10. Beware of possible confusion between *un-* and the combining form *uni*, meaning "one." In which of the following does the prefix *un-* appear?

unissued
unipersonal

unissued

11. In which of the following does the combining form *uni-*, meaning "one," appear?

unison
unimportant

unison

12. If a vote is unanimous, all voters
   are of one mind
   did not vote
   voted one way or the other

                                                    are of one mind

13. On rare occasions, as with *unanimous,* the form may
   suggest the prefix *un-* but the meaning will suggest
   a derivation from the Latin word *unus,* meaning
   "_____."

                                                    one

14. Which of the following words is apparently related to
   unus or *uni-,* meaning "one"?

   unassuming
   unequal
   unique

                                                    unique

15. Obviously most, but not all, words beginning with *un-*
   contain that prefix. Of the following, which word does
   contain that prefix?

   uncivil
   uncle
   unction

                                                    uncivil

16. If a room is not tidy or in good order, it is called

   _____.

                                                    untidy

17. If some fruit is green or immature, it can be called

   _____.

                                                    unripe

18. When you spread a flag out from a furled state, you
   _____furl it.

                                                    *un*furl

19. If something cannot be thought, it is literally
_____able.

*unthink*able

20. A falsehood is the same as an _____.

untruth

21. If a letter lacks an address, it is _____.

unaddressed

22. If one is unwary, heedless, or thoughtless, he is likely
to be _____aware of danger.

*un*aware

23. If something is not of this world or ghostly, it can be
called _____earth_____.

*un*earth*ly*

24. Any writing not in accordance with the rules of grammar is _____.

ungrammatical

25. The middle English *kempen* means "comb." You can
vary that original form to express the idea of uncombed
or un_____ hair.

un*kempt*

Review statement

26. To express a simple negative, a reversal or verb action,
or simply an intensification of action, use the prefix
_____-.

un-

7   *Re* ∽

1. The hardworking prefix *re-* has a mild case of schizo-
   phrenia, with two different meanings. When you return
   something, you give it b_____.

   back

2. When you reread something, you read it a_____.

   again

3. This is not a bad case of split personality, for when you
   reread something, you read it "again" but also go
   "b_____" over it.

   back

4. *Re-* is schizophrenic in still another sense, for it is both
   an active and passive prefix. An active _____ is
   one that can be added to regular words to make new
   words.

   prefix

5. The words *group, heat,* and *load* are words in their
   own right. When you add *re-* you get *regroup, reheat,*
   and _____.

   reload

6. *Re-* is a passive prefix in all words where it is a necessary part and cannot be removed to leave a word.
   Which of the following is not a word when you remove *re-?*

   refer
   readjust
   reuse
   remove

refer

7. *Re-* is a passive prefix or necessary part of which of the
   following words?

   replace
   rerun
   revoke
   react

revoke

8. This distinction helps with the meaning of *re-*, for the
   meaning of the ,active *re-,* as in *reread,* is usually
   "_____," not "back."

again

9. The meaning of the passive *re-,* as in *revert*—when
   you revert to a former habit or practice—is usually
   "_____."

back

10. If *memoir* is a Latin word meaning "mindful," and is
    related to *memory,* when we bring something "back"
    to mind we are said to re_____ it.

re*member*

11. There are several activities which insure better mem-
    ory. One is to view "again" or to _____
    what you want to remember.

review

12. Figures can be cited to show that more can be remembered if one repeats aloud from memory or _____ what he has learned.

recites

13. When you look into a mirror, you see your image _____ed "back."

*reflec*ted

14. If *frenum* is a Latin word meaning "a rein," such as used to curb a horse, to hold yourself "back" from doing something is to _____ from doing it.

refrain

15. If *fugere* is a Latin word meaning "to flee," a shelter or safe retreat to go "back" would be a _____.

refuge

16. If *fundere* is a Latin word meaning "to pour," to repay or "pour back" would be to _____.

refund

17. When you encounter Latin words such as *fugere* and *fundere,* you should habitually drop the last few l_____.

letters

18. If you rescind an order, the prefix suggests that you

    prepared it
    announced it
    read it
    canceled it.

canceled it

19. The *calc* in *recalcitrant* comes from *calx,* the Latin word meaning "heel." This, plus prefix knowledge, should help you define *recalcitrant* as

    cooperative
    forward looking
    stubbornly defiant
    completely helpless

stubbornly defiant

20. *To capitulate* sometimes means "to draw up into heads or chapters." If, at the end, you summarize or briefly outline what you covered, you can be said to

    _____.

recapitulate

21. When you pay a bill, you ordinarily receive something "back" which acknowledges that fact. It is called a

    _____.

receipt

22. All words beginning with *re-* do not contain that prefix. Which of the following does *not* contain a prefix?

    reduce
    reddish
    recur
    result

reddish

23. If the Latin verb *manere* means "to stay," what word means "to stay back"? _____

remain

24. If you are looking for words derived from the Latin verb *mederi,* meaning "to heal," should you look for *med* or *eri?*

med

25. What English word is used to describe the medicine or treatment which "heals" or restores one "back" to health?

remedy

⌐Review statement

26. To recapitulate, the two most common meanings of *re-* are "b_____" and "a_____."

b*ack* and a*gain*

As further review, note the strange words *recant, recidivist, recalcitrant, recondite,* and *replete.* Now apply your knowledge of prefix meaning as you work through the following short test.

1. ____

2. ____

3. ____

4. ____

5. ____

1. *recant*—A) warm up, B) take back, C) speak, D) disagree.

2. *recidivist*—A) backslider, B) politician, C) director, D) pioneer.

3. *recalcitrant*—A) hard, B) powdered, C) shrewd, D) obstinate.

4. *recondite*—A) hidden, B) wise, C) happy, D) old.

5. *replete*—A) completely filled, B) almost finished, C) moist, D) dry.

To *recant* is to take "back" something you have said or believed. A tendency to go "back" to some criminal action or antisocial behavior makes one a *recidivist.* If someone is *recalcitrant,* he tends to kick "back" in an obstinate fashion. If we use words that are too abstruse, we get the meaning hidden or "back" from plain sight. In short, we are *recondite.* After a big dinner you feel full or *replete. Plere* means "fill" and *re-* "again" or "completely."

8 *Trans* ~

1. *Trans-* means "across, beyond, or over." To transport
   a car from New York to San Francisco would be to
   take it a_____ the country.

   across

2. The Latin verb *agere,* meaning "to drive," often comes
   over into English as *act.* If you conduct some business,
   driving it "across" to completion, you can say you
   _____acted it.

   *trans*acted

3. If the Latin noun *mons, montis,* means "mountain,"
   you would expect Monte Carlo to be built on a
   _____.

   mountain

4. A transmontane highway would probably be a road
   o_____ some mountains.

   over

5. If the Latin verb *mutare* means "to change," the
   word which means "change over," as when the al-
   chemists tried to change lead "over" into gold, is
   _____.

   transmute

67

6. In a few words the final *s* of *trans-* is dropped, as in the word meaning a state resembling sleep, as in a hypnotic _____ce.

*tran*ce

7. Pills which take a person from a state of tension "over" to a quiet, calm state are called _____quilizers.

*tran*quilizers

8. Air flights "across" the Atlantic are called _____ flights.

transatlantic

9. If you know that *calere* is the Latin word meaning "heat," you would expect the word *transcalent* to mean "conducting _____ readily."

heat

10. If *ascend* contains a form of *scandere,* "to climb," when you "climb beyond" the limits expected, you can be said to _____ expectations.

transcend

11. If *scribere* means "to write," when you make a written or typed copy of some shorthand notes, you are _____ing them.

*transcrib*ing

12. A copy or reproduction of your academic grades, because it is reproduced "over" on another sheet, is called a _____.

transcript

13. When you change the form of something, you _____ it.

transform

14. In electricity, the apparatus for changing the form of the current from high to low voltage is called a _____.

transformer

15. When blood is transferred from one person to another, it is called a blood _____.

transfusion

16. You would infer that the Latin word *fundere,* found in *transfusion,* probably means

    to rest
    to pour
    to harden.

to pour

17. Someone constantly on the move and without any permanent abode would be called a _____ient.

*trans*ient

18. When someone is transformed in such a way as to exalt or glorify, he is said to be _____.

transfigured

19. If "to go forward" is *to progress* and "to go back," *to regress,* when a man goes "over" set limits so as to break a law or commit a crime, we say he has _____.

transgressed

20. If you know that *lucere* is a Latin word meaning "to shine," you would infer that frosted glass which permits light to shine through would be called _____.

translucent

21. The word meaning to migrate "across" from one country to another would be _____migrate.

*trans*migrate

22. If the prefix *ex-* or *e-* means "out," the word meaning "to migrate out" of a country would be _____.

emigrate

23. What prefix would you add to *migrate* to express the idea of moving *into* a country?

im-
(to make
immigrate)

24. A small window or panel "across" the top of a door is called a _____.

transom

25. Prefix knowledge should suggest that *transpicuous* means something you can

    see through
    listen to
    work at.

see through

Review statement

26. Now you should connect the meanings "across, beyond, or over" with the prefix _____-.

trans-

9 Pro ⌇

1. If *regress* means "to go back," and *egress,* "to go out,"
   "to go forward" would be to make _____gress.

   *pro*gress

2. Apparently, if *progress* means "to go forward," *pro-*
   means "_____."

   forward

3. Another common meaning of *pro-* is "for," in the
   sense of "in favor of." In which of the following words
   is this the meaning of *pro-?*

   produce
   prolabor
   prominent

   prolabor

4. Still a third shade of meaning is "for" in the sense of
   a substitute or "in place of." A word used "for" a
   noun, for example, is a _____noun.

   *pro*noun

5. From now on, whenever you see *pro-,* look for the
   meanings "_____" or "_____."

   forward
   for

71

6. If the Latin *cedere* means "to move or yield" as in *exceed,* what word means "move forward"?

   _____

proceed

7. Prefix meaning should help you define *procephalic* as which part of the head?

   back part
   side part
   fore part
   top part

fore part

8. When a group lines up in a long line and moves in a set fashion down the street, it is called a _____cession.

*pro*cession

9. If the word *claim* comes from *clamere,* meaning "to cry," *exclaim* would literally mean "cry out." What word would mean "cry forth or announce"?

   _____

proclaim

10. Your prefix knowledge should suggest that if someone has a proclivity to vice, he

    shuns it
    tends in that direction
    disclaims it
    hates it.

tends in that
direction

11. A man who serves "for" a consul and has consular authority would be called a _____.

proconsul

12. If *cras* is a Latin word meaning "tomorrow," putting something "forward" to the future would be to _____tinate.

*procras*tinate

13. If an incumbent figure is one which is lying or resting on something, what would you call a figure which is lying "forward," face down? _____

procumbent

14. An extraordinary child, one who has moved "forward" faster than usual, is often spoken of as a child _____digy.

*pro*digy

15. Judging from the prefix, a *proem* is probably

    a poem
    an introduction
    a speech
    a summary.

an introduction

16. If the Latin word *fluere* means "to flow," as in the phrase "fluent speaker," what word probably means flowing "forward"? _____

profluent

17. *Infuse* means "pour in." One who "pours forth" her apologies is _____ in her apologies.

profuse

18. If *inject* means, literally, "to throw in," the word which means to throw forward is _____.

project

19. The word which names an object designed to be thrown or shot "forward" is _____ile.

*project*ile

20. If you lengthen the time, you make it longer or _____ it.

prolong

21. Something remote is literally "moved back." When you "move forward" from one position to a better one, you say you are _____.

promoted

22. If *impel* means "to drive in or into," what word means "drives forward or ahead"? _____

propel

23. Your prefix knowledge should suggest that *propensity* means

    calmness
    thought
    inclination.

inclination

24. If conditions are propitious, they are

    uncertain
    poor
    in favor of
    a hindrance to.

in favor of

25. On a stage, the proscenium is probably

    the front area
    a side area
    the balcony
    the back area.

the front area

26. If *intrude* means literally "to thrust in," what word probably means "to thrust or jut forward"?

protrude

27. Of course not all words beginning with *p, r, o,* have the prefix *pro-*. Which one of the following probably does not contain it?

    proctor
    proscribe
    pronounce
    promise

proctor

Review statement

28. To reiterate—the prefix *pro-* commonly means "f_____ or _____."

forward or *for*

10 *Non*

1. *Non-* is another negative prefix. Compare the words *non-American* and *un-American.* Which one is *less* emphatic and *less* offensive?

   ____

non-American

2. A glance at the words *non-Christian, noncentral, non-Arab,* and *nonacid* suggests that a hyphen is generally used when the base word begins with a ______________ letter.

capital

3. If the *o* in the prefix *non-* is pronounced like the *o* in the word *on,* which of the following pronunciations is correct?

   non-English
   nun-English

non-English

4. If the prefix *non-* is pronounced "non," and the word *none* is pronounced "nun," the way to tell *non-Christian* from *none Christian,* when listening, is to note the difference in pro______________________.

pro*nunciation*

5. Should the first three letters of *nonconductor* be pronounced "non" or "nun"? _______

non

6. *Non-* is often added to a regular word to give us the negative. If a building is "not fireproof," it is, in a word, ———fireproof.

*non*fireproof

7. If one is "not athletic," he is ————————————.

nonathletic

8. If one is "not of age" to do certain things, such as marry or sign contracts, he is in his ———age.

*non*age

9. If *par* means "equal," *nonpareil* probably means "un———————ed."

un*equal*ed

10. You would expect the word *nonillion* to refer to a

waterfall
number
vacuum.

number

11. In law many terms which make useful vocabulary building aids are borrowed directly from Latin. Take the phrase *non compos mentis.* Our word *mental* is derived from *mentis,* which you would infer means ——————— (rhymes with *find*).

mind

12. Adding a two-letter past tense ending to *compos* gives you the English word *compos*———.

compos*ed*

13. If a person's mind is literally not composed or not put together—*non compos mentis*—he is probably mentally

   unbalanced
   alert
   without compare

   unbalanced

14. In logic the term *non sequitur* is applied to an inference that does _____ follow from the premises.

   not

15. If your ego is your self, anything or everything that is "not" the self is _____ego.

   *non*ego

16. The word that means "no entity" is _____.

   nonentity

17. The opposite of *minus* is the word _____.

   plus

18. When we are "not" able to go, speak, or act further or more, we can be said to be completely _____plussed.

   *non*plussed

19. If the Latin word-element *chal* means "to care," the English word meaning "not caring or indifferent" would be _____*ant*.

   *nonchal*ant

20. A substance having "no" nitrogen would be called _____enous.

   *nonnitrog*enous

21. If a person has no distinguishing features or characteristics, if there is literally nothing to describe or "write down" about him, he is non_____script.

   non*de*script

22. A person who is not a resident of a country is a
_____.

nonresident

Review statement

23. As you can see, the prefix *non-,* meaning "_____,"
is relatively easy to manage.

not

Review Exercise II

A. In the blank after each prefix in the left-hand column, write the number, from the right-hand list, of the common meaning of the prefix. The same meaning may apply to more than one prefix. Some meanings will not be used at all.

1. *un-*	_____	1. forward, for
2. *re-*	_____	2. back, again
		3. in, into
3. *trans-*	_____	4. upper
		5. not
4. *pro-*	_____	6. against
		7. across, beyond
5. *non-*	_____	8. one

B. In each of the following sets of words, there is one word which does *not* contain the prefix found in the rest of the words in that set. Using the principles covered in Unit 2, find that word and enter the appropriate letter in the blank at the right.

1. a) untied, b) united, c) unequal, d) unwary   1. _____
2. a) reactor, b) reason, c) receive, d) recess   2. _____
3. a) transfuse, b) transcend, c) translate, d) tramway   3. _____
4. a) proclaim, b) process, c) probe, d) profuse   4. _____
5. a) nonprofit, b)nonentity, c) nonce, d) nonfatal   5. _____

C. Note the phrase in quotation marks in each sentence and express the same idea with a word containing one of the five prefixes in section A.

1. In a word, if a person is "not collegiate" he is _____.
2. If a person is "moving forward" he is making _____.
3. If a person is making a flight "across the Atlantic," he is making a _____ flight.
4. If a person is doing something which is "not expected," he is doing an _____ act.
5. If a person "calls something back," he _____ it.

(*Answers on page 253*)

Vocabulary Review List

Un-	refund	proclivity
uncomfortable	rescind	proconsul
untouched	recalcitrant	procrastinate
uncertain	recapitulate	procumbent
untie	receipt	prodigy
unfasten	remain	proem
unloosed	remedy	profluent
unbroken		profuse
unnoted	**Trans-**	project
unnecessary	transport	projectile
unissued	transact	prolong
unison	mountain	promote
unanimous	transmontane	propel
unique	transmute	propensity
uncivil	trance	propitious
untidy	tranquilizers	proscenium
unripe	transatlantic	protrude
unfurl	transcalent	
unthinkable	transcend	**Non-**
untruth	transcribing	non-American
unaddressed	transcript	non-Christian
unaware	transform	noncentral
unearthly	transformer	non-Arab
ungrammatical	transfusion	nonacid
unkempt	transient	non-English
	transfigure	nonconductor
Re-	transgress	nonfireproof
return	translucent	nonathletic
reread	transmigrate	nonage
regroup	transom	nonpareil
reheat	transpicuous	non compos mentis
reload		non sequitur
revoke	**Pro-**	nonego
revert	progress	nonentity
remember	prolabor	nonplussed
review	pronoun	nonchalant
recite	proceed	nonnitrogenous
reflect	procephalic	nondescript
refrain	procession	nonresident
refuge	proclaim	

11   *Epi* ⌒

1. When *mono-* is added to axial, you get *monaxial.* (Watch that vowel.) In like manner, when you add *epi-* to *axial* you should get _____.

epaxial

2. One variant spelling or form of *epi-* is apparently _____.

ep-

3. Both *mono-* and *epi-* end, not with a consonant, but with a _____.

vowel

4. Both *mono-* and *epi-* are prefixes, not of one syllable, but of _____.

two

5. To generalize, prefixes of two syllables ending in a vowel drop their final vowel when they are added to a root beginning with a _____.

vowel

6. When *mono-* is added to *carp,* you get *monocarp,* a plant that yields fruit only once before dying. In like manner, when you add *epi-* to *carp* you should get _____.

epicarp

7. If you know that the epidermis is the outer layer of your skin, you would expect *epi-* to mean

   under
   middle
   over.

over

8. Yes, *epi-* means "on, upon, over, or on the outside." An inscription "upon" a tomb (*taphos*) is rightly called an _____taph.

*epi*taph

9. A descriptive word or phrase "upon" some person or thing, as "hard-hearted man," is called an _____thet.

*epi*thet

10. A terse, witty statement "upon" some matter is called an _____gram.

*epi*gram

11. The Greek word *demos,* meaning "people," gives us our word *democracy.* A rapidly spreading disease, literally "upon the people," is called an epi_____ic.

epi*dem*ic

12. If a syn*onym* is a word with the same meaning as another word, and an ant*onym,* a word with an opposite meaning, the Greek word *onyma* probably means

   name
   person
   book.

name

13. If you add *epi-* to *onym,* you should get _____; literally, "named on or over."

eponym

14. Since Pennsylvania is named after William Penn (*Penn* coming "over" into *Pennsylvania*), *Penn* is the _____onym of *Pennsylvania*.

*ep*onym

15. Queen Elizabeth is the eponym of the _____an period or age.

*Elizabeth*an

16. The Greeks called the smallest particle an *atom*, meaning "not cut or divisible." Substitute *epi-* for *a-*, add an *e* at the end of the root, and you have the word _____.

epitome

17. With a book or article you can have a complete or a cut or abridged version. Would *epitome*, literally "cut on," refer to the complete or the abridged version?

_____

the abridged version

18. *Epitome* has still another common meaning. In the sentence, "He is the very epitome of health," it apparently means

    opposite
    essence
    enemy.

essence

19. The Greek word *kardia,* as in *cardiogram* or *cardiograph,* apparently refers to what part of your anatomy?

heart

20. The word *epicardium,* then, apparently refers to a layer of tissue "_____ or around" the heart.

on

21. The part of an apple which would most appropriately be called the *epicarp* is the

    pulp
    seed
    stem
    rind
    core.

rind

22. The epicenter of an earthquake would be
    above the place of focus
    in the very middle.

above the place
of focus

23. The Greek word *phyte* means "plant." A geophyte would, therefore, be an earth _____.

plant

24. If *hydrophobia* is an abnormal fear of water, a plant growing only in water would probably be called a _____phyte.

*hydro*phyte

25. If the neoclasical period is the new classical period, a new plant would rightly be called a _____phyte.

*neo*phyte

26. A "new" convert or member, or a novice, is also called a _____phyte.

*neo*phyte

27. A plant that grows "upon" another plant but gets nourishment from the air, as certain mosses, is called an _____phyte—an "upon" plant.

*epi*phyte

Review statement

28. The meanings "on, upon, over, or on the outside" should now be firmly linked to the prefix _____-.

epi-

To fix those meanings more clearly in mind, what word makes your best mnemonic? _____

12 Mis ⌣

1. The prefix *mis-* means "wrong" or "wrongly." If one "plays" a wrong card he _____plays.

*mis*plays

2. Or if, in an engine, a cylinder does not "fire" properly, we say it _____.

misfires

3. If a dress is too large or small and does not "fit" properly, we say it is a _____.

misfit

4. Watch for possible confusion between *miso-* meaning "to hate" and the prefix _____-, meaning "wrong" or "wrongly."

mis-

5. If *gamos* is a Greek word meaning "marriage," someone who "hates marriage" would be a _____gamist, not a misgamist.

*miso*gamist

6. If *gynist* comes from the Greek *gyne,* meaning "woman," a "woman hater" would be a _____.

misogynist

7. If you remember that *neo-* is a combining form meaning "new," you would infer that *misoneism* would mean hatred of _____ things.

new

8. What closely related word would mean "one who hates new things"?

    misoneism
    misoneist
    misoneology

misoneist

9. *Mono-* drops the final *o* when added to a root beginning with a vowel, as in *monaxial.* From this, you could infer that *miso-* added to *anthrope* would give you

_____.

misanthrope

10. Always look after the *s.* If *mis-* is followed by a vowel other than *o,* there is reason to suspect the *shortened* form of _____, meaning "hate."

miso-

11. If one quotes a man incorrectly or wrongly, he _____ him.

misquotes

12. A printing error is usually spoken of as a _____.

misprint

13. If you put or place something in the "wrong" place, you are said to _____ it.

misplace

14. The Latin word *nomen* means "name." At a meeting when you propose someone as an officer, you are said to name or _____ate him.

*nomin*ate

15. Drop the *en* from *nomen* and add *de plume* and you have *nom de plume,* the French phrase for "pen _____."

pen *name*

16. You would infer that a *misnomer* would be a _____ name for something.

wrong

17. To inform someone "wrongly" would be to _____ him.

misinform

18. In *misinform,* the vowel following the *mis-* suggests the possibility of *miso-* in shortened form. A check of meaning, however, shows no idea of the meaning of *miso-,* which is _____.

hate

19. If a book is "wrongly translated" it is _____.

mistranslated

20. If a book is "not" translated it is _____translated.

*un*translated

21. If something is represented "wrongly" it is
_____.

misrepresented

22. An error can also be called a _____.

mistake

23. If money is not used correctly, it is _____.

misused

24. If an actor is "cast" in a role not suited to him, he is
_____.

miscast

25. Prefix knowledge is an aid to spelling also. Always keep the *s* when adding *mis-* to a word. With this in mind, which of the following is spelled correctly?

    mishape
    misshape

misshape

26. Now you need not "spell" a word the "wrong" way and worry about _____ in your letters.

misspellings

Review statement

27. The prefix *mis-* should now bring to mind the means "w_____ or _____ly."

wrong, wrongly

What word will best serve as your mnemonic aid for remembering meaning? _____

13   *Ob* ⌁

1. As you know, an obnoxious person is

   sleepy
   objectionable
   suspicious.

   objectionable

2. When you know that *noxious* comes from a Latin word, you should also know that *obnoxious* contains the prefix

   o-
   ob-
   obn-
   obno-.

   ob-

3. Usually an obstinate person is not *for* a change but a_____ it.

   a*gainst*

4. Similarly, an obstacle is something that does not facilitate your forward progress but works _____ it.

   against

5. Apparently, a common meaning of the prefix *ob-* is

   behind
   against
   beside
   far.

   against

6. For another meaning of *ob-*, think of *objective*. When you have a goal or objective, do you try to go "to or toward" it or "away" from it?

to or toward

7. "To or toward" is apparently another common meaning of the prefix _____-.

ob-

8. Now for the most important principle of all in dealing with prefixes. In the word *assimilate,* the second and third letters are

   different
   alike.

alike

9. One meaning of *assimilate* is "to make like." If one culture is assimilated by another, it is made _____ the other culture.

like

10. When one letter is _____ by another, it is made like it.

assimilated

11. Why this change? Which of the following is an easier combination of letters to pronounce?

   obpress
   oppress

oppress

12. When *ob-* is added to *press,* the *b* in *ob-* is assimilated or made like the letter __ in *press.*

p

13. Judging from the word *occlude,* before roots beginning with *c,* you would expect the *b* in *ob-* to assimilate to a __.

c

14. If *offer* also contains an assimilated form of *ob-*, before roots beginning with an *f* you would expect the *b* in *ob-* to become an ___.

f

15. Now you know that *op-, oc-,* and *of-* are all assimilated forms of the prefix _____-.

ob-

16. However, you should note that when you add *ob-* to *mit,* you drop the *b* completely, to make the word ___*mit.*

*o*mit

17. Judging from this example, you drop the final *b* only when adding *ob-* to a root beginning with the letter ___.

m

18. To aid in spotting assimilative changes, remember *oppress, occlude,* and *offer.* In all three words the second and _____ letters are identical.

third

19. The sign of the doubled consonant, as in *offer, assimilate,* and *effort,* suggests the presence of an assimilated form of some _____.

prefix

20. Remembering a common meaning of *ob-,* you would define an opponent as one who is playing _____ you, not for you.

against

21. Some people are agreeable. Others are fixed and unyielding and can be called ___stinate.

*ob*stinate

22. If a horse is obstreperous, the prefix suggests he is

    quiet
    slow
    unruly.

unruly

23. Your prefix knowledge should help you define the word
    objurgate as to

    sing loudly
    denounce strongly
    praise highly.

denounce
strongly

24. With principles of assimilation in mind, which of the
    following words does not contain the prefix *ob-* in any
    of its variant forms?

    occur
    ocellus
    offend
    opprobrium

ocellus

25. Prefix knowledge should suggest that a speech of
    obloquy would be a speech of

    censorship
    greeting
    farewell.

censorship

26. If a man is obsessed by some fixed idea, that obsession
    works _____ his having a well-rounded per-
    sonality.

against

27. Do not forget assimilative principles when you write the antonym of *defensive,* which is _____.

offensive

28. *To obfuscate,* judging from the prefix, is

    to state
    to encourage
    to explain
    to confuse.

to confuse

29. Using prefix meaning, the word *oppugn* probably means

    open
    assail
    cooperate
    succeed.

assail

Review statement

30. As a review, remember that "against, to or toward" are the common meanings of the prefix _____-.

ob-

31. Remember also the principle of assimilation which most commonly means that the last letter in the prefix is changed to be the same as the first letter in the r_____ which follows, when the letter in question is a consonant.

root

14   *Ex* ⌒

1. If *exclude* means "to keep someone out," and an exile is one who is turned out of his own country, *ex-* apparently means "_____."

out

2. "Beyond" is still another meaning of *ex-*. When you are excessively tired, you are not weary in an average way, but are tired b_____ the average.

beyond

3. In the words *expel* and *eject,* the prefix meaning which seems uppermost is

   out
   beyond.

out

4. The meaning "former or previous" is still another to be noted. In which of the following words does this meaning appear?

   exhale
   extreme
   ex-wife

ex-wife

5. When the prefix *ex-* means "former or previous," it is usually joined by a hyphen to the second part of the word. Therefore, would the word for "former convict" be written *ex-convict* or *exconvict*?

-----

ex-convict

6. There is possible confusion between the Greek prefixes *exo-* and *ecto-* and the prefix _____-, meaning "out."

ex-

7. Fortunately both *exo-* and *ecto-* have the same common meaning as *ex-*, the meaning "_____."

out

8. *Ex-* has a few assimilated forms to watch out for. Just as *ob-* added to *fer* resulted in *offer*, so *ex-* added to *fort* gives us _____.

effort

9. Just as *ob-* becomes *o-* before *mit*, to make *omit*, so *ex-* before *mit* becomes ___-.

e- (emit)

10. The final *x*, however, is dropped not only before *m* but also before *b, d, g, l, n, r,* and *v*. Which of the following is correct?

    elect
    ellect
    exlect

elect

11. Use a pronunciation rule-of-thumb to help determine what form is most likely when prefix and root elements are joined. For example, which is easier to pronounce —exvolve or evolve? _____

evolve

12. With a very few words, the *ex-* is assimilated to *ec-* or
es-, as in _____*centric* and _____*cape.*

*ec*centric
*es*cape

13. Be on the alert for an *e-, ef-, ec-,* or *es-,* all variant or
assimilative forms of the prefix _____-.

ex-

14. When you are completely worn "out," we can say you
are _____hausted.

*ex*hausted

15. A fireman can distinguish himself by putting "out" a
fire or ex_____ it.

ex*tinguishing*

16. When you efface all traces of some action, you wipe
"_____" all traces of it.

out

17. Out of causes you have the inevitable _____fects.

*ef*fects

18. If an intern lives "in" a hospital as a resident doctor,
a doctor who is affiliated with a hospital, but lives
"outside" it, is called an _____.

extern

19. When a dentist pulls "out" one of your teeth, he is
said to ex_____ it.

ex*tract*

20. Remembering the principles of assimilation, if an influx is a "flowing in," a "flowing out" would be called an _____.

efflux

21. If *rupt* comes from a Latin word meaning "to break," "to break out," as lava from a volcano, would be to _____.

erupt

22. When everyone is pulled out of a besieged or threatened city, they are e_____ed.

evacuated

23. If, through court action, a landlord puts a tenant "out," he is said to __vict him.

evict

24. When you put "out" some energy to do some work, you _____ert yourself.

exert

25. Your knowledge of prefixes should suggest that if a book is expurgated, parts of it are

    added
    removed
    poorly written
    rewritten.

removed

26. Use your knowledge of prefixes to define *expatiate*. It probably means

    to conserve
    to threaten
    to enlarge.

to enlarge

27. You would expect *exogamy* to mean marriage

    with an older person
    outside the tribe or clan
    between relatives.

outside the tribe
or clan

Review statement

28. Now whenever you see the prefix *ex-,* remember the meanings "_____, beyond, former or previous."

out

As further review, apply your knowledge of *ex-* in the following test. Since some three thousand new words edge their way into our language every year, it pays to know the indispensable shortcuts. *Over a thousand words* of desk dictionary size, for example, contain a form of *ex-*. You can be sure that many new words will make use of that old element also.

1. If you saw an *egress,* what should you do—
   A) shoot it, B) photograph it, C) go out,
   D) hop on board?   1. _____

2. *elide*—A) play, B) add, C) sew, D) leave out.   2. _____

3. *ebullient*—A) bubbling, B) durable, C) bulb-
   shaped, D) quiet.   3. _____

4. *excaudate*—A) buried, B) without tail, C) short,
   D) full of dirt.   4. _____

5. *eclectic*—A) eulogistic, B) poetic, C) diseased,
   D) selective.   5. _____

When you progress, you go forward; when you regress, you go back. When you *egress,* you go "out." When you pronounce *February,* you should not elide or leave "out" the first *r.* Her ebullient personality marked her out in any group; she bubbled "out" with *ex*citement and enthusiasm. That is the species without any tail—*ex-* (out) + *caudate* (tail). An eclectic approach is one which takes the best "out" of several approaches, which makes it selective.

15   Dis ᕬ

1. *Dis-* has only two variant forms or disguises. Just as *ob-* added to *fer* gives *offer*, so *dis-* added to *fer* gives
   _____.

differ

2. There is only one other variant besides *dif-* (used only before *f*). Just as *ex-* added to *vict* gives *evict,* so *dis-* added to *vert* should give _____.

divert

3. Generally, before roots beginning with *b, d, g, v, m, n, l,* and *r,* the *s* in *dis-* is dropped completely. *Dis-* plus *late* should normally give you _____.

dilate

4. From now on, watch for *dif-* and *di-*, the only two assimilated forms of the prefix _____-.

dis-

5. One meaning of *dis-* is "not," as in the word *dishonest* or "_____" honest.

not

101

6. In addition to its negative meaning, *dis-* also means "separation," as in *dismiss* and *disperse* where *dis-* means

   with or together
   apart or away
   down.

apart or away

7. Thus in a laboratory when an animal is dissected for study it is cut a_____.

a*part*

8. When someone distributes handbills to pedestrians, he does not keep them but gives them _____.

away

9. Beware of possible confusion between *di-,* a prefix meaning "two," and *di-,* a variant form of the prefix _____-.

dis-

10. If a *dilemma* is defined as "a choice between equally disagreeable alternatives," the presence of *di-,* meaning "_____," is suggested.

two

11. With some words, meaning will not help, as with *divide.* If you divide an apple you may cut it in "two" or cut it "a_____."

a*part*

12. *Vulge* comes from a Latin word meaning "common people." What word probably means to make known to the people or to "part" with some information?

   _____

divulge

13. The opposite of *honest* is *dishonest*. The opposite of *harmony* is *disharmony* or _____*cord*.

*dis*cord

14. To persuade is to get someone to do or believe something. The word _____*suade* probably means to turn someone "away" from a course of action.

*dis*suade

15. In a hotel, if you wish to sleep in the morning, just hang a sign on the door, "Do not _____."

disturb

16. When an army officer sends a message "away," he is said to _____*patch* it.

*dis*patch

17. If the Latin verb *sociare* means "to join," the word meaning to "sever associations" would be to _____ yourself.

disassociate

18. If *sipate* comes from a Latin word meaning "to throw," a man who throws or wastes "away" his energies and substance could be said to _____ them.

dissipate

19. If a bear lodged in a tree is driven "away," he is _____.

dislodged

20. When you leave on board a ship, you embark on a trip. When you return and land, you do not embark, you _____.

disembark

21. Your knowledge of prefixes lets you know that when money is disbursed it is

parted with
accepted
saved
counted.

parted with

22. Judging from the prefix, the noun *dishabille* probably means

casually dressed
formally attired
completely dressed
partially dressed.

partially dressed

23. If a girl is diffident, she is probably

sociable
shy
faithful
polite.

shy

24. When there is no middle ground, you either like something or _____ it.

dislike

25. The reverse of *illusion* is *"not"* *illusion* or _____.

disillusion

26. If a married couple decides to part and go separate ways, they usually get a _____.

divorce

Review statement

27. The two meanings of *dis-* to keep in mind are "_____" and "apart or away."

not

The more experience you have in word analysis and in applying your newly acquired knowledge of prefix meaning, the more useful this approach becomes. Keep the meanings "away" and "not" in mind as you try to deal with the following difficult words.

1. _____

2. _____

3. _____

4. _____

5. _____

1. If you're *diffident,* you're A) quarrelsome, B) shy, C) friendly, D) careful.

2. If you *disparage* something, you A) rearrange it, B) extol it, C) replace it, D) belittle it.

3. *discursive*—A) speaking, B) scholarly, C) deserving, D) wandering.

4. *distrain*—A) to draw tight, B) to pretend, C) to travel, D) to take something away.

5. *discommode*—A) serve, B) oppose, C) disturb, D) supply.

If a person is diffident, he tends to stay "away" from the center of things—to withdraw. The dictionary tells us that diffident comes from *dis* + *fidere* (to trust). When we have no trust in ourselves, we are shy or diffident. Add *com-* to *fidere* and you have to "trust together," or *confidence.* Obviously increasing your word power means more confidence and less diffidence. If something is disparaged, it is belittled—something is taken "away" from it. A discursive account tends to wander "away" from the point. Distrain is a legal term for describing the seizing of property as security for some debt. In short, you take "away" some property until the claim is settled, a move which may discommode the owner and take "away" from his peace of mind.

Review Exercise III

A. In the blank after each prefix in the left-hand column, write the number, from the right-hand list, of the common meaning of the prefix. The same meaning may apply to more than one prefix. Some meanings will not be used at all.

1. *epi-* _____		1. apart, not
		2. above
2. *mis-* _____		3. out, beyond
		4. wrong
3. *ob-* _____		5. within
		6. upon
4. *ex-* _____		7. against
5. *dis-* _____		8. near, by

B. In each of the following sets of words, there is one word which does *not* contain the prefix found in the rest of the words in that set. Using the principles covered in Unit 2, find that word and enter the appropriate letter in the blank at right.

1. a) epigram, b) epicritic, c) epilogue, d) epic   1. _____
2. a) misinform, b) misery, c) misstatement, d) miscue   2. _____
3. a) obsolete, b) obelisk, c) offend, d) occlude, e) oppress 3. _____
4. a exit, b) egress, c) efflux, d) extrabold   4. _____
5. a) dismiss, b) disjunctive, c) diffuse, d) divert, e) digitate 5. _____

C. Use your knowledge of prefixes to help you deal with the relatively strange words in the following vocabulary test. Enter the appropriate letter in the blank at the right.

1. *eparch* means a) old person, b) ruler over a province, c) loyal individual, d) traveler   1. _____
2. *misfeasance* means a) surface, b) substitute, c) spokesman, d) wrongdoing   2. _____
3. *objurgate* means a) speak against, b) agree with, c) judge, d) juggle   3. _____
4. *effete* means a) feminine, b) courageous, c) worn out, d) difficult   4. _____
5. *disburse* means a) pay out, b) take in, c) burden, d) improve   5. _____

(*Answers on page 253*)

Vocabulary Review List

Epi-
epaxial
epicarp
epidermis
epitaph
epithet
epidemic
epigram
epitome
epicardium
epicarp
epicenter
epiphyte

Mis-
misplay
misfire
misfit
misogamist
misogynist
misoneism
misoneist
misanthrope
misquote
misprint
misplace
misnomer
misinform
mistranslate
misrepresent
mistake
misuse
miscast
misshape
misspelling
Ob-

obnoxious
objectionable
obstinate
obstacle
objective
oppress
occlude
offer
omit
opponent
obstreperous
objurgate
obloquy
offensive
obfuscate
oppugn

Ex-
exclude
exile
excessively
expel
eject
ex-wife
ex-convict
effort
emit
elect
evolve
eccentric
escape
exhausted
extinguishing
efface
effect
extern

extract
efflux
erupt
evacuate
evict
exert
expurgate
expatiate
exogamy

Dis-
differ
divert
dilate
dishonest
dismiss
disperse
dissect
distribute
divide
divulge
disharmony
discord
dissuade
disturb
dispatch
disassociate
dissipate
dislodge
disembark
disburse
dishabille
diffident
dislike
disillusion
divorce

16 In 🙐

1. If *insecure* means "not secure" and *insane* means "not sane," you would infer that *in-* means "_____."

   not

2. *In-*, however, has an identical twin *in-* which must be remembered. One *in-* means "in or into," the other means "_____."

   not

3. *To assimilate* is "to make similar or like." When *in-* is added to *literate,* the *n* is assimilated by the *l* to give _____*literate* or "not" literate.

   *il*literate

4. When *in-* is added to a root beginning with *r,* you have the same kind of change: *in-* plus *ruption* gives the word _____.

   irruption

5. A labial sound is one made mainly by motion of the lips. Which one of the following letters requires the lips in pronouncing—*l, m, n,* or *t?* ___

   m

6. Before the labials *m, p,* and *b, in-* becomes *im-,* as in
____*partial.*

*im*partial

7. The ease-of-pronunciation check is useful. Sound each
letter distinctly. Which of the following is somewhat
easier to pronounce?

   immortal
   inmortal

immortal

8. The other labials *p* and *b* have the same effect. Which
is easier to pronounce, the first or second in each of
these pairs?

   impossible *or* inpossible
   imbalance *or* inbalance

the first
(*impossible* and
imbalance)

9. This useful negative prefix helps us condense two words
into one, to turn, for example, "not vulnerable" into
_____*vulnerable.*

*in*vulnerable

10. The Latin word *volo* means "willing." When we do
something unwillingly or accidentally, we may be said
to do it _____untarily.

*invol*untarily

11. If an object is out of sight and "not" visible, we would
call it _____.

invisible

12. If *validus* is a Latin word meaning "strong," one
who is not strong but sick and weakly is called an
_____.

invalid

13. If *utilis* is a Latin word meaning "useful," the word *inutile* probably means "_____ useful."

not

14. Our word *urban* as opposed to *rural* is derived from the Latin word *urbs,* which you would infer means

    city
    country.

city

15. Since city people were thought to be more smooth and polished in manner, the adjective *urbane* came into our language, derived from the Latin word _____, meaning "city."

urbs

16. If someone is *inurbane* he

    lacks polish
    is impractical
    is carefree
    acts on impulse.

lacks polish

17. If *trepid* comes from a Latin word meaning "alarmed," you should expect *intrepid* to mean

    cowardly
    fearless
    weary
    wise.

fearless

18. If a man is "not" tolerant, he is, in a word, _____.

intolerant

19. In which of the following words do you have the prefix *in-,* meaning "not"?

    intend
    intemperate
    inductive
    invite

intemperate

20. If something can "not" be suffered, it is
_____.

insufferable

21. If *flammable* means "burnable," you might expect
inflammable to mean "_____ burnable."

not

22. But *inflammable* contains the other prefix *in-* and actually means easily set "in" flames or burnable. This
suggests the danger of confusing the *in-* meaning "not"
with the *in-* meaning "_____."

in

23. If an act is "not" legal, it is, in a word,
_____.

illegal

24. If *legere* is a Latin word meaning "to read," you would
expect legible writing to be writing which could be
_____.

read

25. If someone's writing is "not" legible or readable, you
would call it _____.

illegible

26. If the results are not capable of being measured, you
would call them _____measurable.

*im*measurable

27. If you favor no one side or party more than another,
you are indeed a fair and _____partial critic.

*im*partial

28. When, in a discussion, a speaker makes a point which
   is "not" relevant, we call it an _____
   remark.

                                                irrelevant

Review statement

29. Remember that *il- im-,* and *ir-* may be assimilated
   forms of the prefix _____-.

                                                    in-

17 Com ∽

1. To discover what *com-* means, think of words beginning with *com-,* such as *combine, compress,* and _____*pile.*

*com*pile

2. Now look more closely at *combine* and *compress.* If you combine the necessary ingredients to make a cake, you do not keep them separate; you mix them t_____.

to*get*her

3. Now you can use other words beginning with *com-* to check the assumption that *com-* means "together." When you compress something into smaller space, you press it more tightly "_____."

together

4. You can see that *com-* means "together or with." But that knowledge is not as useful as it should be unless you can identify all the as_____ed forms of *com-*.

as*similat*ed

5. Remember the common meaning of *assimilate* ("to make like"). You would, with that definition in mind, expect *com-* plus *lision* (from *laedere*, "to strike") to result in the word _____*lision*.

*col*lision

6. Similarly, when adding *com-* to a root beginning with *r* such as *respond*, you would expect *com-* plus *respond* to lead to _____*respond*.

*cor*respond

7. Just as with certain other prefixes, the assimilative change is a dropping of the final consonant. When adding *com-* to *education* (a root beginning with a vowel), you get _____*education*.

*co*education

8. *Com-* also drops its *m* before roots beginning with *h* or *w*, which means *com-* plus *here* gives you _____*here*, not *comhere*.

*co*here

9. Only one other assimilative change exists: the change of *m* to *n* before roots beginning with *c, d, f, g, h, q, s, t,* and *v,* as in _____*cept*.

*con*cept

10. Do not rely on rote memory. Use the pronunciation rule of thumb to bring you to the appropriate change from *comrode* to _____*rode*.

*cor*rode

11. Not *conlect* but _____*lect* is correct.

*col*lect

12. And not *comoperate* but _____ is correct.

cooperate

13. If *trahere* means "to draw," the name of a legal device for drawing two or more parties "together" on some agreement is _____tract.

*con*tract

14. If *nectere* means "to fasten," when you bring two wires "together," you are said to _____ them.

connect

15. If *preempt* means to "buy before," the word which would probably mean to buy the entire supply "together" is _____empt.

*co*empt

16. If *inherent* means literally "sticking into," the word which probably means "sticking together" is

_____.

coherent

17. Now use your prefix knowledge to help you define *collate* as

    to compare
    to read
    to remedy
    to delay.

to compare

18. If you "labor with" someone on a writing project, you _____laborate with him.

*col*laborate

19. A colleague of yours is probably a

    neighbor
    fellow worker
    manager
    stranger.

fellow worker

20. If *bat* is a root derived from the Latin word meaning "to beat or fight," the English word meaning "to fight with" would be _____.

combat

21. If you are asked to serve with others on some project, the group is usually called a _____mittee.

*com*mittee

22. If you remember that *panis* is a Latin word meaning "bread" and that breaking bread "together" is an ancient rite of friendship, you see where we got the word _____*panion*.

*com*panion

23. The members of a church are sometimes spoken of as a flock, a meaning derived from the Latin *gregare,* "to gather in a flock." That in turn gives us our word

_____.

congregation

24. If *progress* is "stepping forward," and *regress,* "stepping back," the word which literally means "stepping together" is _____.

congress

25. If the Latin *sequi* means "to follow," that which follows as a result of something is called a _____sequence.

*con*sequence

26. If the Latin word *tangere* means "to touch," when one person gets in touch "with" another, he is said to _____ him.

contact

27. Watch for possible confusion between *contra-* meaning "against" and *con-,* an assimilated form of *com-.* Which one of the following words does not contain a form of *com-?*

    contribute
    control
    convention
    contradict

contradict

Review statement

28. The common meanings of *com-* are "with" or "_____."

together

29. The four variant forms are *col-, con-, cor-,* and _____-.

co-

For further review, apply your prefix knowledge to the words in the following test.

1. ____

2. ____

3. ____

4. ____

5. ____

1. If a word is labeled *colloquial* in the dictionary, does that mean it is A) substandard, B) vulgar, C) incorrect, or D) conversational?

2. *compeer*—A) look, B) associate, C) sightseer, D) nobleman.

3. *complot*—A) conspiracy, B) criminal, C) story, D) garden.

4. *conjugal*—A) matrimonial, B) judicial, C) military, D) personal.

5. *contiguous*—A) unfavorable, B) touching, C) spreading, D) angular.

With well over a thousand words of desk dictionary size containing a form of the prefix *com-,* it is a particularly useful shortcut to word meanings. The words *loquacious, eloquent,* and *elocution* are all derived from *loqui,* meaning "to speak," as is true with *colloquial,* literally "to speak together," as in conversation. A colloquialism is, therefore, proper to casual conversation. A compeer is someone we associate "with" on a fairly equal basis. Since conspiracies are usually the work of several people, when you plot "with" someone that becomes a complot. The words *conjugal, junction, juncture, join,* and *conjunction* all have a form of *jungere,* meaning "to join." When two people are joined "together" as man and wife you have a conjugal relationship, a state of matrimony. When two things touch, they are "together," hence contiguous.

18   Sub ∽

1. Since you know that a submarine runs under water, you will have no trouble remembering that *sub-* means
   "_____."

under

2. While the idea of "under, beneath, below" is perhaps the most common meaning, *sub-* also means "lower in rank or position." If there are agents and subagents, the subagents are _____ in rank or position than the agents.

lower

3. Your dictionary mentions still other meanings for the idea of "under"—such as "to a lesser degree than, somewhat, slightly." In which of the following words is that meaning dominant?

   subdivided
   subhuman

subhuman

121

4. After learning the meaning, you must learn how to identify *sub-* in actual words. With *sub-*, this means recognizing seven variant forms. Just as *dis-* plus *fer* equals *differ*, so *sub-* plus *fer* would equal _____*fer*.

*suf*fer

5. This change of the last letter in *sub-* to the first letter of the root is most common. For example, before *g* as in *gest*, *sub-* would become _____-.

sug-

6. And before *m*, as in *mon*, *sub-* becomes _____-.

sum-

7. This same pattern holds when you add *sub-* to *ceed* to get _____*ceed*, under in rank, secondary, or subordinate.

*suc*ceed

8. Try pronouncing the combinations both ways as a further check. Which of the following is easier to say distinctly?

   subplant
   supplant

supplant

9. Before an *r*, as in *render*, *sub-* combines to make _____*render*.

*sur*render

10. One other somewhat different change occurs: *sub-* sometimes becomes *sus-* before a *p, t,* or *c*. Therefore, when you add *sub-* to *pend*, you get _____*pend*, not *suppend*.

*sus*pend

11. From the following words, see if you can pick the one which does not contain the prefix *sub-*.

   supply
   suspect
   supreme
   surrogate

                                          supreme

12. The third step—the payoff—is using this knowledge effectively in arriving at word meanings. For example, *sonic* comes from a Latin word meaning "sound." When we travel at sonic speed, we travel at the speed of _____.

                                          sound

13. When a plane passes the sonic barrier, it exceeds the speed of sound or travels at super_____ speed.

                                          super*sonic*

14. Of course, the majority of us still travel at speeds "under" those of sound, or _____sonic speeds.

                                          *sub*sonic

15. We are conscious of many things but some of our mental activity is "under" our conscious level and is therefore called _____conscious.

                                          *sub*conscious

16. When a nation is *subjugated,* the prefix suggests that it is

   brought under control
   set free
   disorganized.

                                          brought under
                                          control

17. Action designed to overthrow the established order is well described by the word meaning literally "to turn under," a _____versive action.

*sub*versive

18. If *fer* comes from *ferre*, meaning "to bear," when pain bears you "under," you are said to _____.

suffer

19. If you impress a friend with the need to keep certain facts "under" cover, you try to _____ those facts.

suppress

20. When you doubt or distrust someone, you tend to look "under" the surface because you _____pect him.

*sus*pect

21. When the water from a big wave sinks or falls, it is said to _____side.

*sub*side

22. When light is diffused it is "poured in every direction." When light is suffused it is overspread—literally, "poured _____."

under

23. The last step—to generalize—is a reminder that by studying a few elements carefully we can learn about others also. If *merge* comes from a Latin word meaning "to plunge," our word meaning "to plunge under" would probably be _____.

submerge

24. Now if you remember the prefix meaning "out," you should know that the word meaning "to plunge out" would be ___*merge.*

*e*merge

25. And if you know the prefix meaning "in," you will know that the word meaning "to plunge in" would be _____*merge.*

*im*merge

26. Generalizing again, suppose there were a prefix *hub-*. If it were combined with the root *rain,* which of the following combinations would it make?

hubrain
hurrain
hurain
hubbain

hurrain

Review statement

27. When you see *suf-, sug-, sum-, suc-, sup-, sur-,* and *sus-,* remember that you may be seeing a variant or assimilated form of the prefix _____-.

sub-

When you learn to apply one prefix element that un-locks the meanings of over a thousand common English words you have, in a sense, stepped up your vocabu-lary-building efforts to supersonic speed. Lean on your knowledge of *sub-* in taking the following difficult test.

1. ____

2. ____

3. ____

4. ____

5. ____

1. If you're told to get a *subaltern,* you should start looking for A) a calibrated barometer, B) a handwriting expert, C) a part for a gasoline engine, or D) someone of inferior rank.

2. *subliminal*—A) below the threshold of conscious-ness, B) a projecting appendage, C) limitless, D) terminal.

3. *submontane*—A) monetary, B) monastic, C) be-neath a mountain, D) a ravine.

4. *subsume*—A) dig out, B) spend lavishly, C) put under the proper heading, D) begin all over again.

5. *succinct*—A) exact, B) concise, C) tight, D) juicy.

A *subaltern* is "under" someone else in rank. As you might expect, the root *altern* comes from the Latin word *alter,* meaning "other," as in our words *alter ego, alternate, alter,* and *altercation.* Subliminal is a tech-nical word from psychology which describes sensations which are not consciously perceived, hence are under the level of conscious awareness. Submontane is, of course, "under" a mountain. And when you classify information under a heading, you subsume it—from *sub* + *sumere* (to take), as in our words *assume, con-sume,* or *resume.* If something is succinct, it is said with an "under" supply of words, not an oversupply.

19   *In* ~

1. *In-* and *in-*, the identical twins of the prefix world, are found in over 2,000 English words of a desk-sized dictionary. One *in-* means "not," the other "in or into." In which of the following words do you have *in-* meaning "in or into"?

    infirm
    inside
    inactive

    inside

2. In which of the following words do you have *in-*, meaning "not"?

    intrude
    investigate
    invisible

    invisible

3. You have only three variants to note, *ir- il-,* and *im-.* If *to assimilate* is "to make similar," you would expect *in-* plus *lustrate* to give _____*lustrate.*

    *il*lustrate

4. Before *regular* you would expect *in-* to become _____*regular* or not regular.

    *ir*regular

127

5. Which one of the following letters does *not* require bringing the lips together in its pronunciation—*p, m, n,* or *b*?

n

6. Before the labials *p, m,* and *b* the prefix *in-* becomes *im-*, as in ____*bibe.*

*im*bibe

7. If you are alert, you build a vocabulary just from reading. From the last two items, for example, you would infer that labials are letters articulated mainly by the _____.

lips

8. In words of English origin, such as *land, in-* is usually unchanged, giving us the form ____*land.*

*in*land

9. *In-* has a French form *en-*. If you close something "into" a letter you either inclose or ____close it.

*en*close

10. Just as *in-* plus *bue* equals *imbue,* so *en-* plus *brace* would give ____*brace.*

*em*brace

11. Remember the meaning check. For example, which of the following words does *not* have the meaning "in or into"?

    encircle
    enclose
    embrace
    emerge

emerge

12. Sometimes the meaning "to make, or cause to be" is uppermost. In which word is this meaning dominant?

    enfeeble
    enthrone

enfeeble

13. One may migrate into or out of a country. The prefix makes the difference. Add *in-* to *migrate* and you get the word meaning "to migrate into," "_____."

immigrate

14. Add an assimilated form of *ex-*, meaning "out," to *migrate* and you get ___*migrate,* meaning "to migrate out."

*e*migrate

15. If explosion is a bursting "out," an implosion would be a bursting "_____."

in

16. If you have an automobile tire you can either deflate or _____flate it.

*in*flate

17. The Latin word *lumen* means "light." Light coming "into" a room will i_____ate it.

i*llumi*nate

18. The Latin verb *rigare* means "to water." When water is channeled "into" fields to supply moisture for crops, we call it _____ing.

*irriga*ting

19. The first line of a paragraph is usually set in from the margin or _____dented.

*in*dented

20. The Latin noun *pes, pedis,* means "foot." When your foot gets entangled "in" something so as to hinder your progress, we say it _____pedes progress.

*im*pedes

21. Then when you get your foot "out," your progress is
    _____pedited.

*ex*pedited

22. Use prefix meaning in defining an impetuous person as
    one who

    enjoys things
    rushes into things
    damages things.

rushes into
things

23. The new evidence uncovered by detectives tended to
    _____plicate another man.

*im*plicate

24. The opposite of *export* is _____.

import

25. When the president is formally inducted "into" office
    he is _____augurated.

*in*augurated

26. When a surgeon operates, he usually makes an
    in_____.

in*cision*

27. To inculcate something on your mind is to

    impress
    calculate
    read
    forget it.

impress

28. When you invest some money you can take re-
    sulting loss or decrement, or the opposite—a gain or
    _____.

increment

Review statement

29. To recapitulate, the prefixes *in-* and *in-* mean "_____"
    and "_____ or _____."

                                                not, in or into

30. The variant forms *ir-, il-,* and *im-* may be forms of the
    prefix _____-.

                                                in-

20 Ad ～

1. The common meaning of *ad-* is "to or toward." If *imply* means "fold in," and *reply,* "fold back," the word which literally would mean "fold to" is *ap_____.*

2. *Ad-* is the most changeable prefix in the English language. Remember that *assimilate* means "to make similar." When you add *ad-* to a root beginning with *p* you get _____-, as in _____ply.

3. Try pronouncing *adclaim* rapidly and you will be reminded that before a *c, ad-* becomes _____-.

4. If *ad-* becomes *ac-* before a *c,* you would expect *ad-* to become _____- before a *g,* as in _____*gravate.*

5. Before a root beginning with *f,* you would expect an assimilative change in *ad-,* as in_____*fliction.*

133

6. If she has a smile that lures men to her, there is reason to call her _____luring.

*al*luring

7. And before an *n,* you would expect *ad-* to become _____-, as in _____*notation.*

an-

*an*notation

8. Before an *r,* the assimilated form of *ad-,* _____-, would appear, as in _____*rest.*

ar-

*ar*rest

9. The word which both names and illustrates the variant changes you are now studying is the word _____*similate.*

*as*similate

10. Before a root beginning with a certain consonant, the *d* in *ad-* is assimilated or made like that consonant; for example, *ad-* plus *tract* makes _____*tract.*

*at*tract

11. One other type of assimilative change occurs before a root beginning with *sc, sp,* or *st*—the final *d* is dropped—as when adding *ad-* to *scend* to make ___*scend.*

*a*scend

12. With ten variant forms, *ad-* is not always easy to spot. With all but the last variant, however, the sign of the double consonant will help you determine which words contain a form of *ad-*. Which of the following does not contain *ad-*?

   attempt
   arrive
   appease
   apology

apology

13. Such words as *affinity, aggrieve, alliance,* and *annex* all contain evidence, the sign of the _____ consonant, for suspecting the presence of *ad-*.

double

14. Another rule-of-thumb check is the prefix-substitution check. In which word can you substitute another prefix?

   apply
   apple

apply (to make
reply, comply,
or *supply*)

15. The meaning check is still another to remember. In which of the following words is the meaning "to or toward" strongest?

   advance
   adrift

advance

16. With the *a-* form of *ad-*, watch for possible confusion with the Greek prefix *a-*, meaning "not" which is different from *ad-*, meaning "_____ or toward."

to

17. For example, which of the following words contains the Greek prefix *a-* (meaning "not")?

   atypical
   aspect

atypical

18. With prefix meaning in mind, you would infer that the strange word *adit* probably means

   an approach or entrance
   a farewell or parting
   a number.

an approach or
entrance

19. Judging from the prefix, the strange word *adnate* probably means

   lowered
   hindered
   separated
   joined.

joined

20. From the prefix meaning "to" and the root *nectere,* "to tie or bind," comes our word describing an addition to a building—an _____*nex*.

*an*nex

21. When riches flow in great abundance "to" someone, he is rightly called wealthy or _____fluent.

*af*fluent

22. When you support something, calling others to accept your point of view, you are _____vocating its support.

*ad*vocating

23. If a regressive move is a move "back," an _____ move would mean a move "to or towards."

aggressive

24. Remember, you can either reject or _____cept an idea.

*ac*cept

25. If a prefix is added "before" the root and a suffix "after," both are added "to" the root and are therefore _____fixes.

*af*fixes

26. When you bring people to a certain spot, you may be said to _____semble them there.

*as*semble

27. When you lay out a lesson or indicate a task, you are said to _____sign it.

*as*sign

Review statement

28. Whenever you see *ap-, ac-, ag-, af-, al-, an-, ar-, as-, at-* or just plain *a-,* remember it may be a form of the prefix _____-, the most changeable prefix in the English language.

ad-

Review Exercise IV

A. In the blank after each prefix in the left-hand column, write the number, from the right-hand list, of the common meaning of the prefix. The same meaning may apply to more than one prefix. Some meanings will not be used at all.

1. *in-* _____		1. away
		2. not
2. *com-* _____		3. near
		4. together, with
3. *sub-* _____		5. under
		6. into
4. *in-* _____		7. to, towards
5. *ad-* _____		8. up

B. In each of the following sets of words, there is one word which does *not* contain the prefix found in the rest of the words in that set. Using the principles covered in Unit 2, find that word and enter the appropriate letter in the blank at the right.

1. a) indigo, b) import, c) irradiate, d) illustrate   1. _____

2. a) collaborate, b) comic, c) correspond, d) cooperate,
   e) converge   2. _____

3. a) succinct, b) sustain, c) support, d) suffuse, e) submerge,
   f) sully   3. _____

4. a) incurable, b) infallible, c) ideal, d) illiterate,
   e) irrational   4. _____

5. a) approach, b) accord, c) aggressive, d) after, e) attract,
   f) assist, g) arrange, h) allocate   5. _____

Use your knowledge of prefixes to fill in the blanks below.

1. If *regress* is to "step back," an entrance or place to "step in" would be an ___gress.

2. If *ingress* is a place to "step in or into," a place to "step out" would be an exit or ___gress.

3. If an *egress* is a place to "step out," when you "step toward" someone as if to fight, you are acting ___gressively.

4. If *aggressive* means "stepping to or toward," when a formal assembly comes to "step together," it is rightly called a _____gress.

5. If you now forget that *gress* means to "step," you will be taking a "step back" or ___gressing, instead of _____gressing.

(*Answers on page 253*)

Vocabulary Review List

In-
insecure
insane
illiterate
irruption
impartial
immortal
impossible
imbalance
invulnerable
involuntarily
invisible
invalid
inutile
inurbane
intrepid
intolerant
insufferable
inflammable
illegal
illegible
immeasurable
impartial
irrelevant

Com-
combine
compress
compile
collision
correspond
coeducation
cohere
concept
corrode
collect
cooperate
contract
connect
coempt

coherent
collate
collaborate
colleague
combat
committee
companion
congregation
congress
consequence
contact

Sub-
submarine
subagent
subhuman
suffer
suggest
summon
succeed
supplant
surrender
suspend
subsonic
subconscious
subjugated
subversive
suppress
suspect
subside
suffused
submerge

In-
inside
illustrate
imbibe
inland
enclose
embrace

immigrate
implosion
inflate
illuminate
irrigating
indent
impetuous
implicate
import
inaugurate
incision
impress
increment

Ad-
apply
acclaim
aggravate
affliction
alluring
annotation
arrest
assimilate
attract
ascend
affinity
aggrieve
alliance
annex
advance
adit
adnate
affluent
advocating
aggressive
accept
affix
assemble
assign

Review Essay

As a further means of sharpening awareness of contextual clues and as a review of all prefixes studied in this text, fill in the blanks with the appropriate prefixes. The common meaning of the prefix is given in the margin. You are not asked to identify *all* prefixes. When words with prefixes are repeated, they are not always structured with blanks to be filled.

Notice as you work through this selection how prefix knowledge helps you both understand and remember words more readily. For example, induction is by derivation a leading "in" to a generalization. Given certain facts, you use them to lead you "into" a generalization. When you move "away" from a general law to an individual case or situation, you are said to deduce certain things about it.

Suppose you notice that a prelude is something played before a service and that a postlude is something played after. With those two instances in mind, when you reason that *lude* probably means "play," what process did you use to arrive at that conclusion —induction or deduction? Obviously most of the frames in this text encourage you to use methods of reasoning and scientific investigation in learning and using words and word parts.

All Men Are Scientists *

Thomas Henry Huxley

Scientific —vestigation is not, as many people seem to ——pose, some kind of modern black art. You might easily gather this —pression from the manner in which many persons speak of scientific —quiry, or talk about —ductive and —ductive philosophy, or the principles of the "Baconian philosophy." I do ——test that, of the vast number of cants in this world, there are none, to my mind, so ——temptible as the pseudo-scientific cant which is talked about the "Baconian philosophy."

To hear people talk about the great Chancellor—and a very great man he certainly was, —you would think that it was he who had —vented science, and that there was no such thing as sound reasoning before the time of Queen Elizabeth! Of course you say, that cannot possibly be true; you ——ceive, on a moment's —flection, that such an idea is —surdly wrong. . . .

into
under
into

into/into
away
forward

together, with

into

through
back, again/away

* From *Darwiniana*, 1893.

141

out

before/out
apart, not

together, with
through/apart, not
together, with

apart, not
together, with
not

to, toward

out, beyond
back, again
in
away

together, with
together, with
for/to
to/before

together/apart

apart
to

The method of scientific investigation is nothing but the ___pression of the necessary mode of working of the human mind. It is simply the mode at which all phenomena are reasoned about, rendered _____cise and ___act. There is no more _____ference, but there is just the same kind of difference, between the mental operations of a man of science and those of an ordinary person, as there is between the operations and methods of a baker or of a butcher weighing out his goods in _____mon scales, and the operations of a chemist in _____forming a _____ficult and _____plex analysis by means of his balance and finely-graduated weights. It is not that the action of the scales in the one case, and the balance in the other, _____fer in the principles of their _____struction or manner of working; but the beam of one is set on an ___finitely finer axis than the other, and of course turns by the ___dition of a much smaller weight.

You will understand this better, perhaps, if I give you some familiar ___ample. You have all heard it ___peated, I dare say, that men of science work by means of ___duction and ___duction, and that by the help of these operations, they, in a sort of sense, wring from Nature certain other things, which are called natural laws, and causes, and that out of these, by some cunning skill of their own, they build up hypotheses and theories. And it is imagined by many, that the operations of the _____mon mind can be by no means _____pared with these _____cesses, and that they have to be ___cquired by a sort of special _____nticeship to the craft. To hear all these large words, you would think that the mind of a man of science must be _____stituted _____ferently from that of his fellow men; but if you will not be frightened by terms, you will _____cover that you are quite wrong, and that all these terrible ___paratus are being used by yourselves every day and every hour of your lives.

There is a well-known __cident in one of   into
Molière's plays, where the author makes the
hero __press __bounded delight on being told   out/not
that he had been talking prose during the whole
of his life. In the same way, I trust, that you will
take ____fort, and be __lighted with yourselves,   with/down
on the discovery that you have been acting on
the principles of __ductive and __ductive   in/down
philosophy during the same period. Probably
there is not one who has not in the course of
the day had __casion to set in motion a   against
____plex train of reasoning, of the very same   with
kind, though ____fering of course in degree, as   apart
that which a scientific man goes through in trac-
ing the causes of natural phenomena.

A very trivial circumstance will serve to
__emplify this. Suppose you go into a fruiterer's   out
shop, wanting an apple,—you take up one, and,
on biting it, you find it is sour; you look at it,
and see that it is hard and green. You take up
another one, and that too is hard, green, and
sour. The shopman offers you a third; but, before biting it, you __amine it, and find that it is   out
hard and green, and you __mediately say that   into
you will not have it, as it must be sour, like
those that you have already tried.

Nothing can be more simple than that, you
think; but if you will take the trouble to analyse
and trace out into its logical elements what has
been done by the mind, you will be greatly sur-
prised. In the first place, you have ____formed   through
the operation of __duction. You found that, in   in
two __periences, hardness and greenness in   out
apples went together with sourness. It was so in
the first case, and it was ____firmed by the   together
second. True, it is a very small basis, but still it
is enough to make an induction from; you generalize the facts, and you __pect to find sour-   out
ness in apples where you get hardness and
greenness. You found upon that a general law,
that all hard and green apples are sour; and that,
so far as it goes, is a ____fect induction. Well,   through

144 PREFIX REVIEW ESSAY

against	having got your natural law in this way, when you are __fered another apple which you find is hard and green, you say, "All hard and green apples are sour; this apple is hard and green, therefore this apple is sour." That train of reasoning is what logicians call a syllogism, and has
before	all its various parts and terms—its major _____-
before/together, with	mise, its minor ____mise, and its ____clusion. And, by the help of further reasoning, which, if drawn out, would have to be __hibited in two
out	or three other syllogisms, you __rive at your
forward	final __termination, "I will not have that ap-
down	ple." So that, you see, you have, in the first place, established a law by induction, and upon that you have founded a deduction, and reasoned out the special conclusion of the par-
under	ticular case. Well now, _____pose, having got your law, that at some time afterwards, you are
apart	_____cussing the qualities of apples with a friend: you will say to him, "It is a very curious thing,— but I find that all hard and green apples are sour!" Your friend says to you, "But how do you
back, again	know that?" You at once __ply, "Oh, because I have tried them over and over again, and have always found them to be so." Well, if we were talking science instead of common sense, we
out	should call that an __perimental verification.
against	And, if still __posed, you go further, and say, "I have heard from the people of Somerset- shire and Devonshire, where a large number of
against	apples are grown, that they have __served the same thing. It is also found to be the case in Normandy, and in North America. In short, I
out	find it to be the universal __perience of man-
to/apart	kind wherever __tention has been __rected to
under	the _____ject." Whereupon, your friend, unless
not/to	he is a very __reasonable man, __grees with you,
together	and is _____vinced that you are quite right in
together	the _____clusion you have drawn. He believes,
through	although _____haps he does not know he be-
out	lieves it, that the more __tensive verifications
out	are,—that the more frequently __periments

have been made, and ___sults of the same kind   back
___rived at,—that the more varied the _____-   to/together
ditions under which the same results are___-   toward
tained, the more certain is the ultimate conclusion, and he _____putes the question no   against
further. He sees that the experiment has been
tried under all sorts of conditions, as to time,
place, and people, with the same result; and he
says with you, therefore, that the law you have
laid down must be a good one, and he must
believe it.

In science we do the same thing;—the
philosopher ___ercises _____cisely the same   out/before
faculties, though in a much more ___licate man-   down, away
ner. In scientific inquiry it becomes a matter of
duty to ___pose a _____posed law to every pos-   out/under
sible kind of verification, and to take care, more-
over, that this is done ___tentionally, and not   into
lcft to a mere ___cident, as in the case of the   to, towards
apples. And in science, as in common life, our
_____fidence in a law is in ___act _____portion   with/out/forward
to the ___sence of variation in the result of our   away
experimental verifications. For ___stance, if you   in
let go your grasp of an article you may have in
your hand, it will ___mediately fall to the   into
ground. That is a very _____mon verification of   together, with
one of the best established laws of nature—that
of gravitation. The method by which men of
science establish the ___istence of that law is   out
___actly the same as that by which we have   out
established the trivial _____position about the   forward
sourness of hard and green apples. But we believe it in such an ___tensive, thorough, and   out
___hesitating manner because the universal ___-   not/out
perience of mankind verifies it, and we can
verify it ourselves at any time; and that is the
strongest possible foundation on which any
natural law can rest. . . .

Part III Roots

21 Capere 〜

1. In English as in Latin, verbs have a variety of forms. We say, "I run," "You run," "He run___."

run*s*

2. Fill in the correct form of the verb *run* in the following sentence. "I was _____ down the street."

running

3. Some forms are made by adding letters, as in *runs* and *running*. Others involve internal change, as in the sentence, "Yesterday he r___n home."

r*a*n

4. The infinitive form is made in still another way, by adding a *to* before the verb, giving us the form "_____ run."

to

5. The infinitive form, with the *to* either understood or expressed, is the form we use in talking about a verb. We therefore speak of the verb *run* (*to* is understood) or the verb _____ *run*.

to

149

6. With Latin verbs, most infinitive forms end in *-ere,*
   -are, or *-ire.* If the Latin verb *capio* means "I take,"
   the form *capere* probably means "____ take."

to

7. To help spot English words derived from Latin verbs,
   drop the infinitive ending to get the base form. For
   example, the base form of *capere* would be _____.

cap

8. Since our word *capture* contains *cap,* you have
   reason to suspect it is derived from the Latin verb
   _____, meaning "to take or seize."

capere

9. Go a step farther, however. Always check form with
   meaning. Does the word *capture* contain the idea of
   "taking or seizing"? _____

yes

10. *Capture* appears related to *capere,* "to take or seize,"
    in both form and _____.

meaning
(or idea)

11. Finally, a glance at the dictionary will corroborate
    the fact that *capture* is derived from the Latin verb
    _____.

capere

12. Thinking in terms of these rule-of-thumb checks, which
    of the following two words is derived from *capere*?

    captivity
    capstone

captivity

13. Now put this useful shortcut to use. A small, soluble, gelatin container designed to "take" or enclose a dose of medicine is called a _____sule.

*cap*sule

14. If a man has real ability to "take" charge, we speak of him as competent or _____, literally, "able to take."

capable

15. If someone spoke of a capacious container, you would assume it would _____ a lot to fill it.

take

16. Because it "takes" your attention, the heading, title, or subtitle, as of a picture, is called a _____tion.

*cap*tion

17. As with English verbs, be alert to discover variant forms. For example, when you accept something, you _____ it from the donor.

take

18. The *cept* in *accept* is very similar to the *capt* in *capture,* the kind of change we see in *run* and *ran.* Furthermore, *accept* and *capture* both obviously contain the idea of _____ or seizing.

taking

19. A glance at *accept* in the dictionary lets you know that it is actually derived from the Latin verb _____, "to take or seize."

capere

20. Alert yourself to variations in English words. When a man practices a deception on someone, he is said to de＿＿＿＿＿＿ him.

de*ceive*

21. Use the chain reaction of analogy to extend understanding. *Deceive* is to *deception* as *receive* is to ＿＿＿＿＿＿＿＿＿＿.

reception

22. What related form of *deceive* and *deception* means "tending to deceive"? ＿＿＿＿＿＿＿ful

*deceit*ful

23. When you receive an award, you are a re＿＿＿＿ient of it or the one who "takes" it.

re*cip*ient

24. If you are the recipient of money, you may be asked to give a written acknowledgment that you "took" it, something for the donor to "take" as proof of delivery. This is called a re＿＿＿＿＿＿.

re*ceipt*

25. Always look for the idea of "taking." If someone "takes" your attention because of her beauty and charm, you have reason to call her ＿＿＿＿tivating.

*cap*tivating

26. If you find a case that does not follow the general rule, you call it an ex＿＿＿＿＿＿ion because you have to "take" it out of the general category and deal with it separately.

ex*cep*tion

27. In a school, the one who "takes" top place in authority is called the school prin_____.

prin*cipal*

28. When you take part in some activity, you are a parti_____ant.

parti*cip*ant

Review statement

29. Although *cep, cip, ceiv, ceipt,* and *ceit* are possible variant forms of *capere,* the most common form to note is the form _____.

cap

22   *Ponere* ⌐

1. *Ponere,* "to put or place," makes an important contribution to English. Dropping the infinitive *-ere* gives
you the form most commonly found in English, the
base form _____.

pon

2. If an article is made by "putting" several parts together,
you can speak of them as com_____ent parts.

com*pon*ent

3. The number 3 in x^3 is a figure that is "put" above
and out to the right and is, therefore, called an
ex_____.

ex*pon*ent

4. Someone pitted against you in a contest or game is your
op_____.

op*pon*ent

5. When *pon* comes at the end of a word, with no suffix
following, you usually add a final *e,* as in the word
meaning "to defer or *put* off until later"—the word
post_____.

post*pone*

6. Now let your knowledge of English lead you to another form of *ponere*. An opponent is not on the same side as you but on the op_____e side.

op*posit*e

7. Sometimes, as with *opposite,* there is an *e* added. At other times you have no *e*. For example, when you go to the bank to "put" some money into your account, you de_____ it.

de*posit*

8. If a man wants employment—a "place" for himself— he may try to find a _____ion with the government.

*posit*ion

9. When you "put" words together, as when writing themes in school, you call the result a com_____.

com*position*

10. If you know the two-letter prefix meaning "out," you should be able to build the word meaning to "put out" information, explain, or make clear. "He wrote a brilliant _____ion on relativity."

*exposit*ion

11. Remember what happens to *in-* when it is followed by *p*? If you do, you will know that when one person "puts" himself "in" another person's way without right or invitation, it is an _____.

imposition

12. Think of the prefix meaning "before." Look at the phrases "in the road" and "by her." Since such words as *in* and *by* are usually "put before" a noun or pronoun, they are called _____.

prepositions

13. When you transform 592 to 529, you have made a
trans_____ of the 9 and the 2.

trans*position*

14. A man can be indefinite about some things, but sure
or _____tive about others.

*posi*tive

15. By now whenever you see a *pon, pone, posit,* or *posite*
you should think of *ponere,* meaning "to _____ or
_____."

put
place

16. Do not stop here, though. Let us see if you can discover still another variant. When there is a transposition of two numbers, we can say they have been
trans_____.

trans*posed*

17. As with *pon,* which sometimes is *pone,* so it is with
pos, which is sometimes _____.

pose

18. Yes, when you drop the *it* from *posit,* you get the
variant form _____.

pos

19. When a man makes an offer of marriage, we say he
made a _____ of marriage.

proposal

20. For another variant, suppose we turn to the farmer. When he "puts" up a fence, he usually begins by putting _____ at certain intervals along a line.

posts

21. Yes, *post* is another common variant. It is found in a word meaning a fraud who deceives by pretending to be someone that he is not, or an im_____.

im*postor*

22. And remember, when you "put or place" a stamp on a letter, that stamp is called a _____ stamp.

postage

23. (Be careful not to confuse *post-*, the prefix meaning "behind or after," and *post*, a variant form of the Latin verb _____.)

ponere

24. When a person stands erectly we say he has good _____ure.

*post*ure

25. When you "put" leaves, vegetable refuse, and the like "together" for subsequent fertilization of the soil, you call it a com_____ pile.

com*post*

26. In chemistry when you "put" two or more elements "together" and mix them, you have a *compound*. You would infer from meaning that *pound* is probably a variant of the Latin verb _____.

ponere

27. When someone "puts" forth some pet notions or ideas of his on a subject, he is said to pro———————— them.

pro*pound*

28. By now you can begin to see how many of our English words are derived from *ponere,* meaning "to ———————— or ————————."

put
place

29. Now you should be better able to deal with such difficult words as *juxtaposition* which means

   side by side
   moving along slowly
   falling rapidly.

side by side

30. When you spot a form of *ponere* in the word *juxtaposition,* you are ready to say it means "to put or place *juxta,* or ———————— by ————————."

side
side

Review statement

31. The two most common three-letter combinations from *ponere* are ———————— and ————————, with *pound* and *post* also to be noted.

pon and *pos*

23   *Tenere* ⌒

1. The Latin verb *tenere* means "to have or hold." *Tenio*
   is the first person singular, present tense, and means
   "I ⎯⎯⎯⎯ or ⎯⎯⎯⎯."

have
hold

2. The *-ere* in *tenere* indicates the infinitive form. To get
   the form most frequently seen in English, drop the
   three-letter infinitive ending, leaving ⎯⎯⎯.

ten

3. The third person singular, present tense, of *tenere* is
   found by dropping the infinitive ending and adding
   the ending *-et,* giving us the word ⎯⎯⎯⎯⎯.

tenet

4. *Tenet*—the Latin word meaning "he holds"—comes
   over into English without change to mean "a principle
   or doctrine ⎯⎯⎯ by someone or some group."

held

161

5. Now for some English derivatives. When you "hold" on firmly and stubbornly, you hold on _____aciously.

*ten*aciously

6. When someone won't let go easily, we say he "holds" on with bulldog _____acity.

*ten*acity

7. The officer who "holds" the authority in lieu of the captain is called a lieu_____.

lieu*tenant*

8. One who, as a renter, "holds" a room, apartment, or house, is spoken of as a _____.

tenant

9. An apartment building, since it is intended to "hold" a number of different families may be spoken of as a _____ement house.

*ten*ement

10. When teachers have worked in a school system for a set period of time, their "hold" on the position is considered permanent and they are said to have _____ure.

*ten*ure

11. In military language, a position that can be "held" is called a _____able position.

*ten*able

12. To discover variant forms, take English words that you already know, such as the word *de*_____*tion*.

de*ten*tion

13. You would not say, "Don't let me detention you any longer," but you would say, "Don't let me de_____ you."

detain

14. This shows that you recognize *tain* as another form of the Latin verb _____.

tenere

15. This opens the way to a whole new family of words. *Detention* is to *detain* as *retention* is to _____.

retain

16. If a drinking glass "holds" some milk, we say it _____ milk.

contains

17. If the facts are relevant, they can be said to per_____ to the matter in question.

per*tain*

18. If he is supported or "held" from below, he is sus_____ by someone.

sus*tained*

19. It is with food that we all main_____ life.

main*tain*

20. When you hold out hospitality to someone, inviting him to your house, you are said to enter_____ him.

enter*tain*

21. If *ab-* or *abs-* means "away," when you "hold" yourself "away" from smoking you are said to _____.

abstain

22. If you abstain completely, this is spoken of, not as total *abstainence,* but as total *abs*_____*ence.*

ab*stin*ence

23. In this way your knowledge of English brings you to *tin* as still another variant from the Latin verb _____.

tenere

24. If you read of a man's pertinacity, you would expect him to "_____" on with persistence.

hold

25. When something "holds" the same pattern over a period of time, we say it has con_____ued in that way for that time.

con*tin*ued

26. A large and extensive land mass (something "held" together) is often spoken of as a con_____ _____.

con*tinent*

27. Now whenever you see a *ten, tent, tain, tin,* or *tinu* in a word, look for the idea of "having or _____."

holding

28. A word of caution. Beware of possible confusion between *tendere,* "to stretch," and *tenere,* "to _____ or _____."

have
hold

Review statement

29. The forms *ten, tain,* and *tin* are all common forms from the Latin verb _____.

tenere

24 Ducere ∽

1. The Latin verb *ducere,* "to lead," comes over into English without the *-ere* sign of the infinitive, giving us the base form _____ to watch for.

duc

2. If a certain setting "leads" to or contributes to a feeling of restfulness, we can say it is con_____ive to rest.

con*duci*ve

3. To reinforce root meanings, always try to use them when dealing with derivatives. For example, with *conducive,* from *ducere* ("to lead"), think of a situation conducive to learning as one "_____" you in that direction.

leading

4. Some think *education* is a pouring in of information, but the word itself means literally "to _____ out."

lead

5. A silent *e* after *duc* is common. For example, when someone goes on a special diet to lure away excess poundage, we say he is trying to re_____.

reduce

165

6. If a company manufactures cars, it literally "leads them forward," or pro_____ them.

produces

7. When you produce a picture one or more times, as in printing, you are said to re_____ it.

reproduce

8. Your root knowledge should let you infer that the Italians called Mussolini *Il Duce* because he was their _____.

leader

9. Now call on your knowledge of English to lead you to a common variant. When you introduce someone, you make an intro_____ion.

introduction

10. If a man encourages or "leads" a girl to give up her chastity, we say he se_____ her. And if anything is tempting or strongly attractive we can speak of it as seductive.

seduces

11. Some men are by title "leaders" in their country. To get the title, change the *c* in *duce* to *k* to make _____.

duke

12. Still another variant is introduced when a duke marries, for his wife then becomes a _____ess.

duchess

13. For still another variant, think of how electric wires are "led" through walls. For that purpose a metal tube, either rigid or flexible, called a con_____, is used.

con*duit*

14. Now that you know the variant forms *duc, duct, duk, duch,* and *duit,* let's take a closer look. A man who "leads" a group on a tour is called a tour con_____.

con*ductor*

15. Something that is produced is known as a pro_____.

pro*duct*

16. If your vocabulary development is facilitated by studying roots of words, we can call this a pro_____ive method.

pro*duct*ive

17. A copper wire is able to carry or _____ electricity.

conduct

18. If an aquatic plant is a water plant, you would call a conduit for bringing water from a distant source an aque_____.

aque*duct*

19. If *viatic* means "of a road," the word describing a structure to carry a road over a valley or gorge would be a _____.

viaduct

20. A pliant, easily bent metal strip is _____ile in nature.

*duct*ile

21. With root meaning in mind, if a detective educed important information from a suspect, he would probably

    lose it
    draw it out
    pass it by
    discover it.

draw it out

22. To reason from the known down to the unknown is called de_____ive reasoning.

de*duct*ive

23. The opposite, reasoning from the particular to the general, is called in_____ reasoning.

in*ductive*

24. Using root knowledge, you would expect *adduce* to mean

    to remain still
    to bring in reasons
    to be confused.

to bring in
reasons

25. And you would surmise that *to traduce* would be

    to take away character
    to fear discovery
    to disagree with.

to take away
character

Review statement

26. Although *duit, duke, duct, duch,* and *duce* are all possible derivatives of *ducere,* the most common form is

_____.

duc

25   *Mittere* ~

1. When the three-letter sign of the infinitive is dropped from *mittere,* "to send," the base form _____ remains.

   mitt

2. In English words derived from *mittere,* look for the idea of "sending." For example, the radio on the ship kept "sending" out or trans_____ an SOS signal.

   trans*mitting*

3. Or when your car is "sending" out smoke through the exhaust you can say it is e_____ smoke.

   e*mitting*

4. If you decide to attend a play you must first buy a ticket ad_____ you to the theater to see the performance.

   ad*mitting*

5. If a sound is sent periodically, starting and stopping at intervals, it is not continuous but inter_____ent.

   inter*mitt*ent

6. When a group is "sent" to work together on some matter, you ordinarily call them a com_____.

com*mittee*

7. Suffixes change words. If you agree to complete this assignment, you have to "send" yourself through it. We say you have com_____ yourself to do it.

com*mitted*

8. Of course, sometimes a *t* is dropped off the *mitt* to give us the variant *mit,* as in the phrase you might see on a ticket—"_____ one."

ad*mit*

9. Since *mittere* means "to send" and *ad-* means "to," *admit* means literally "_____ to."

send

10. If you forget something or neglect to do it, you can be said to o_____ it.

o*mit*

11. When someone yields to another he literally "sends himself under" or sub_____ himself to another's wishes.

sub*mits*

12. After you receive a bill, you send money back for payment, or re_____ the money.

re*mit*

13. If you consent to something or allow it, you can be said to per_____ it.

per*mit*

14. Again, let your knowledge of English lead you to an important variant form. You would not say "the admit price was high" but that "the ad_____ price was high."

admission

15. If the United States "sends" out an agent or messenger on some specific mission, he is often spoken of as our e_____ary.

e*miss*ary

16. When a painter agrees to paint a certain picture, we say he is com_____ to do it.

com*missioned*

17. A man sent on a mission by his church to preach in a foreign country is called a _____.

missionary

18. That part of your car which transmits force from the engine to the wheels is called the t_____.

transmission

19. If a man is careless or negligent at work, or if he holds back from doing what he should, we call him re_____.

re*miss*

20. A weapon designed to be "sent" by throwing or shooting is appropriately called a m_____.

m*issile*

21. With the variant *miss,* the final *s* is sometimes dropped and replaced by an *e,* as in the word *pro*_____.

pro*mise*

22. Now put your knowledge of roots to work. As a definition of *missive,* consider which of the following is closest to the idea of "sending."

    a letter
    a magnet
    an error
    a heavy object

a letter

23. With the action "send" in mind, you would infer that the strange word *remise* probably means

    to judge
    to hesitate
    to surrender
    to stop.

to surrender

24. You would infer that *manumit* probably means

    to cut or sever
    to injure
    to light
    to set free or send away

to set free

Review statement

25. Now when you see a *mitt, mit, miss, mis,* or *mise,* you have strong reason to suspect a word derived from the useful Latin verb *mittere,* meaning "to _____."

send

Review Exercise V

A. In the blank after each root in the left-hand column, write the number, from the right-hand list, of the common meaning of the root. The same meaning may apply to more than one root. Some meanings will not be used at all.

1. *capere* _____	1. have, hold	
	2. open	
2. *ponere* _____	3. send	
	4. take, seize	
3. *tenere* _____	5. stretch	
	6. put, place	
4. *ducere* _____	7. lead	
	8. bring	
5. *mittere* _____		

B. From each group of words, select the one word whose meaning is most like that of one of the roots in section A. Enter the appropriate letter in the blank at the right.

1. a) capsize, b) capacity, c) capillary, d) caper   1. _____
2. a) posture, b) posse, c) posterior, d) possible   2. _____
3. a) tenth, b) tennis, c) tenderize, d) tenant   3. _____
4. a) conduct, b) duplicate, c) dunce, d) duckling   4. _____
5. a) missile, b) mitten, c) missus, d) misspell   5. _____

C. Note the phrase in quotation marks in each sentence and express the same idea with a word containing a form of one of the roots in section A.

1. "Take-out" as in the sentence, "All went home _____ Bill."
2. "Put-down" as in "_____ your money in the nearest bank."
3. "Hold-back" as in "Will you _____ the same classification when you go to the other college?"
4. "Lead-in" as in "The government will _____ more men in the next draft call."
5. "Send-out" as in "The car was _____ smoke from the exhaust."

(Answers on page 253)

Vocabulary Review List

Capere
capture
captivity
capsule
capable
capacious
caption
accept
deception
deceive
receive
reception
deceitful
recipient
receipt
captivating
exception
principal
participant

Ponere
component
exponent
opponent
postpone
opposite
deposit
position
composition
exposition
imposition
preposition
transposition
transpose
proposal
post
impostor
postage
posture

compost
compound
propound
juxtaposition

Tenere
tenet
tenaciously
tenacity
lieutenant
tenant
tenement
tenure
tenable
detention
detain
retention
retain
contain
pertain
sustain
maintain
entertain
abstain
abstinence
pertinacity
continue
continent

Ducere
conducive
education
reduce
produce
reproduce
Il Duce
introduction
seduce
seductive

duke
duchess
conduit
conductor
product
productive
conduct
aqueduct
viaduct
ductile
educe
deductive
inductive
adduce
traduce

Mittere
transmitting
emitting
admitting
intermittent
committee
committed
admit
omit
submit
remit
permit
admission
emissary
commission
missionary
transmission
remiss
missile
promise
missive
manumit

26   *Scribere* ∾

1. To remember that *scribere* means "to write," associate it with the common word *describe,* which means "to _____ down information about a person or thing."

write

2. The dictionary definition of *describe* is "to tell or write about." As a better mnemonic, visualize a famous "writer" vividly de_____ some unusual character.

de*scribing*

3. As might be expected, the most common form of *scribere* is found by dropping the *-ere,* leaving the base form _____.

scrib

4. For a word that means "writer, clerk, penman, or secretary," add an *e* to the preceding base form to make the word _____.

scribe

5. If a man "writes" carelessly or illegibly, we say he _____bles.

*scrib*bles

6. If you "write" your name at the end of a paper to indicate support or approval, you are said to sub_____ to the proposition.

subscribe

7. When some words or letters are written or engraved into a metal plate, we say they are in_____ on it.

inscribed

8. When a secretary puts her shorthand notes into readable English, we say she tran_____ them.

transcribes

9. If an old play is thought to be "written" by a certain author, we say it is attributed or a_____ to that writer.

ascribed

10. You should now be alerted to *scribere* and its meaning, "to _____."

write

11. Now use your knowledge of English to bring you to a common variant. You do not say, "Give me a describtion," but you say, "Give me a de_____."

description

12. If that description is vivid, it is probably because you made use of some good _____ive terms.

descriptive

13. What word originally meant anything "written" but now usually refers to the Bible? Think of the relationship between *feat* and *feature* to get from *script* to
_____.

scripture

14. Another slightly variant form is derived by dropping the final *t* in *script* to get _____.

scrip

15. The last variant form to note is found by substituting a *v* for the *p* in *scrip* to get the form _____.

scriv

16. With *scrib, script, scrip,* and *scriv* in mind, you have the necessary information to spot words derived from *scribere,* "to _____."

write

17. Now apply that knowledge. You would expect a scriptorium to be a
    reading room
    warehouse
    writing room
    waiting room.

writing room

18. And even without a dictionary you would expect a scrivener to be a
    file clerk
    copyist
    receptionist
    metal worker.

copyist

19. In taking a vocabulary test, if you came to *rescript,* which choice would you select?
    request
    repeat
    copy
    TV rerun

copy

20. In ancient Rome, *proscribe* probably meant
      to publish
      to announce
      to resist.

to publish

21. A scrip is probably a
      pill
      certificate
      merchant
      screen
      scout.

certificate

22. When you write x^2 the 2 is called an exponent or
    super_____.

super*script*

23. Before you buy certain pills, you must have a doctor's
    _____ to take to the drug
    store to be filled.

prescription

24. When you finish a letter then "write" an afterthought
    below your signature, that is called a "P. S." or
    _____.

postscript

25. A compulsory enrollment of men into the armed
    forces is called a con_____ion.

con*script*ion

26. Be sure to cultivate habits of generalizing. If *cir-
    cumvent* means "to come (*venire*) around (*circum-*),"
    circumscribe means literally "to _____
    _____."

write around

27. In the dictionary definition for *circumscribe,* "to trace
    a line around or limit," the word closest in meaning to
    "write" is the word _____.

trace

28. Now you can see how helpful the Latin verb
_____, "to write," is in dealing with
English words.

scribere

Review statement

29. The variants *scrib, script, scrip,* and the less common
scriv are the variant forms to look for from the Latin
verb _____.

scribere

27   *Facere* ∽

1. It takes a skilled word detective to identify *facere,* "to make or do," in all its variant forms. Drop the *-ere* to get the important base form _____.

   fac

2. An exact reproduction—"made" similar to the original —would appropriately be called a _____simile.

   *fac*simile

3. If a craftsman works with real skill and speed, we can call him a _____ile worker.

   *fac*ile

4. A facile craftsman is one who "does" things with genuine _____ility.

   *fac*ility

5. If you are talking about something that is true or was actually "done," just add a *t* to the base form to make the word _____, a variant of *facere.*

   fact

6. A building in which things are manufactured or "made" is sometimes called a _____.

factory

7. If *bene-* means "good or well," a person who helps, often giving financial assistance, is known as a _____.

benefactor

8. If a company "makes" cars, we say it manu_____ them.

manu*factures*

9. What letters do the variants *fac, fact,* and *factur* have in common?

fac

10. Just as *run* and *ran* are forms of the same verb, so *fac* and *fic* are both forms of *facere,* "to _____ or do."

make

11. Which of the following words probably contains a form of *facere*?

   efficacious
   flaccid
   fabulous
   finesse

efficacious

12. Try to generalize about *facere* from your knowledge of *scribere*. If you know that *scrib* and *scribe* are variants of *scribere,* you should expect *fic* and _____ to be variants of *facere.*

fice

13. Using your root knowledge, in which choice is "making or doing" dominant? An *artifice* is a

    necklace
    tall plant
    skill
    artery.

    skill

14. Judging from the *fice,* an *edifice* is probably a

    tree
    wind
    opening
    building.

    building

15. The change of vowel from *fac* to *fic* suggests that *fec* might also be a variant form of _____.

    facere

16. Think of a word with *fec*. A blemish or flaw is, for example, often spoken of as an imper_____.

    imper*fection*

17. *Imperfection* is the condition of not being "_____" perfectly, more evidence that the word is derived from the Latin verb _____.

    made
    facere

18. With root meaning in mind, if you read about an efficacious drug you can see reason for thinking of it as

    costly
    weak
    effective
    harmful.

    effective

19. At first sight you might not expect *fash* to be a variant until you think of a _____ionable article—an article "made" to be in style.

    *fash*ionable

20. You would expect *feat* to be another variant, since an "act or deed of an unusual nature" is actually called a _____.

feat

21. Now change the *t* in *feat* to *s* and add *ible*. If something can be "done," it is indeed _____.

feasible

22. Do not overlook *fit* as still another variant. When someone "does" well by you, it is a real bene_____.

bene*fit*

23. That still does not exhaust the possible variants. A bogus ten-dollar bill is not "made" by the government and is not real money but counter_____ money.

counter*feit*

24. Always corroborate inferences about derivation by checking both form and meaning. In the word *defect*, the letters _____ look like a form from *facere*.

fect

25. Checking the meaning of the word, you see that an article with a *defect* is not "_____" perfectly.

made

26. Your final authoritative check on this and other derivations should be made by consulting your desk _____.

dictionary

Review statement

27. Whenever you see a *fac, fact, fic, feat, feas, featur,* or *fair,* look for the idea of _____ing or doing.

*mak*ing

28   *Tendere* ᔈ

1. *Tendere* means "to stretch." Whenever you suspect a derivative of that Latin verb, be sure to look for the meaning "to _____."

   stretch

2. *Tendere* has only three important variant forms. The first is found by dropping the three-letter infinitive ending to give us the base form _____.

   tend

3. Your knowledge of English will lead easily to the other two. When you attend class, you must give things your full at_____ion.

   at*tent*ion

4. And when you extend credit to someone, that ex_____ion of credit is important.

   ex*tens*ion

5. Now you have all three variants—*tend, tent,* and *tens.* What three letters do they all have in common? _____

   ten

6. Remember the Latin verb *tenere,* "to have or hold"? When you drop the infinitive ending you have _____.

ten

7. Note a significant difference. When *ten* is followed by a *d, t,* or *s,* it is probably from *tendere,* "to _____."

stretch

8. Unfortunately one variant of *tenere* is *tent,* a form identical with a variant from _____, meaning "to stretch."

tendere

9. To resolve such confusions, you must rely heavily on meaning. For example, a piece of canvas "stretched" so as to provide a shelter is called a _____.

tent

10. In which of the following words is the idea of "holding" or "having" dominant?

retention
cxtent

retention

11. In which of the following words is the idea of "stretching" predominant?

retention
extent

extent

12. An added silent *e* to *tens* should not confuse you. If you stretch your muscles tight they are no longer relaxed but _____.

tense

13. Mental or nervous strain, often with muscular taut-
    ness, is spoken of as _____ion.

*tens*ion

14. A wire that can stand a good bit of pull or "stretch" is
    said to have high _____ strength.

tensile

15. If there is an inclination or disposition toward some-
    thing, we call it a _____ency in that direction.

*tend*ency

16. If you have a tendency to do your best work in the
    morning, we can say that you _____ to work best
    at that time.

tend

17. When you have a plan or purpose in mind—literally,
    when you "stretch" yourself "in" a certain direction—
    you can be said to _____ to do something.

intend

18. And when you intend to do something, that becomes
    your _____.

intention

19. A man who supervises a group is often called a
    _____ent.

*superintend*ent

20. When a man claims something falsely or simulates
    illness, he is said to be _____ing.

*pretend*ing

21. When you *pretend* to be something you aren't, you use a word which means, literally, "to _____ before."

stretch

22. When you "stretch" yourself to class, you are said to at_____ class.

at*tend*

23. When you struggle with difficulties—literally "stretch together" with them—you have to con_____ with them.

con*tend*

24. Judging from root knowledge, if a man is ostentatious, he is probably
   quiet
   short
   young
   big-headed.

big-headed

25. In defining *subtend,* which choice is most strongly related to the idea of "stretching"?
   place under
   extend under
   press under

extend under

26. If a sack is distended it is probably
   flattened
   swollen
   small
   brown
   close-woven.

swollen

Review statement

27. When you see a *tend, tent,* or *tens* in a word, suspect the meaning, "to _____."

stretch

29 *Specere* ᕲ

1. The Latin verbs *specere, spectare,* and *spicere* have one thing in common: they all mean "to see or look," as in our word *spectator*—one who _____ or _____.

   sees
   looks

2. Three of the most important forms to look for are found by dropping the infinitive ending from *specere, spectare,* and *spicere* to get the base forms _____, _____, and _____.

   spec
   spect
   spic

3. Cultivate the ability to put across ideas succinctly by using root knowledge. For example, to "look into" matters carefully, as in examining items prior to shipping, would be to _____ them.

   inspect

4. Here is a chance to apply your knowledge of prefixes. Think of the prefix meaning "out." When you are awaiting someone—literally "looking out" for him—you say you _____ him any minute.

   expect

5. When you progress you "step forward." When you retrogress, you "step back." Now as you "look back," your childhood days may seem happy and carefree in retro_____.

retro*spect*

6. In your present position, as you "look ahead," you might say the _____ for advancement are good.

prospects

7. If the *circumference* is the distance "around" a circle, when you "look around" carefully before acting, you are rightly called _____ in your behavior.

circumspect

8. *Extro-* and *intro-* are opposites. If an extrovert is one more interested in others than in himself, one primarily interested in himself would be called an _____.

introvert

9. An introvert tends to "look within" himself at his own feelings and reactions, a process known as intro_____ion.

intro*spect*ion

10. When you have an especially good vantage point for looking things over, for seeing through problems, we say your per_____ive is good.

per*spect*ive

11. If someone deserves your esteem or regard and is someone you can "look" to "again and again," you are said to _____ him.

respect

12. If you know the prefix meaning "to or toward," you can add it to *spect* to get the word that fits this context: "I'm not well acquainted with all parts or _____ of the business."

aspects

13. One who paints is a painter. In the same way, that which is a "visible" disembodied spirit or ghost may be called a _____.

specter

14. Looking back at *specere* and *spectare,* we see that dropping the infinitive endings leaves two forms; the only difference between them is the letter __.

t

15. So far we have looked at words with *spect.* Drop the *t* for the word that fits the following context. When you collect samples of something, you can speak of them as _____imens.

*spec*imens

16. Roots are invaluable in leading you to meaning. Take the strange word *speculum.* Root knowledge should let you know that it means

speech
charm
bill
mirror.

mirror

17. When someone talks about *specious* reasoning, you will note *spec* and infer that this kind of reasoning

is subtle
looks right but isn't
is right
seems involved.

looks right
but isn't

18. People who "watch" games, programs, and the like are known as _____.

spectators

19. Think of the prefix meaning "under" to get the next word. With certain individuals, when you tend to "look" beneath or "under" outward appearances, you are said to distrust or _____ them.

suspect

20. All the English derivatives of the Latin verbs meaning "to see or look" that we have studied so far have contained *spec*. If you drop the infinitive ending from *spicere,* you have _____.

spic

21. Actually your knowledge of English would bring you to *spic*. You would not say you look on him with suspection but with _____.

suspicion

22. When you descend you go "down." When a man "looks down" on someone with contempt or scorn, he _____ him.

despises

23. A character who deserves to be despised is called a _____able character.

*despic*able

24. One who behaves in a despicable manner behaves _____ly.

*despicab*ly

25. If a sponsoring agent or agency is "seeing" to some of the details of a program, we can say it is given under their au_____.

au*spices*

26. If someone "looks" around secretly and furtively to get valuable military information, he is called a ———.

                                                    spy

27. You now have another key to unlock word meanings. If a person is perspicacious, he is probably

    clear-sighted
    obvious
    intelligent
    hot.

                                            clear-sighted

Review statement

28. By now, a *spec* or *spic* should make you think of the meanings "to look or ———."

                                                    see

30 *Plicare* ∿

1. The Latin verb *plicare,* "to fold," has more variant forms than most verbs. To find the obvious one, drop the infinitive ending to get the base form _____.

   plic

2. The verb in Latin also appears in the form *plicatus.* Dropping the *-us* ending gives you another important form, _____.

   plicat

3. To find still a third form, change the *a* in *plicat* to *i,* making _____.

   plicit

4. What letters do the three variants *plic, plicat,* and *plicit* have in common? _____

   plic

5. Sometimes even the *c* is dropped and you have the variant _____ remaining.

   pli

6. Now work through the next items to familiarize yourself with these forms. When you fold a sheet of paper
together several times, you make it more difficult or
com_____ to read.

com*plicated*

7. By this time you are accustomed to seeing a silent *e*
added to some base forms. For example, a partner in
crime goes by the special name of an accom_____.

accom*plice*

8. If some plastic is "foldable" you can also speak of it
as _____able.

*pli*able

9. We say it is not what he said but what he intimated or
im_____ that is most important.

im*plied*

10. When what a man says involves another, we say it
im_____ him in the crime also.

im*plicated*

11. When you make something clear or "unfold" all the
details, you are said to explain or ex_____ ate it.

ex*pli*cate

12. When something is said clearly and distinctly, we say
it was stated definitely or ex_____.

ex*plicitly*

13. When a man begs humbly, he literally "folds" himself
"under" or becomes a sup_____ant.

sup*pli*cant

14. The change from *i* to *y* in *pli* opens up a whole new subfamily as illustrated in _____*wood.*

*pli*wood

15. Add the prefix meaning "together" to *ply* to make a word meaning to "act in accord with a request, demand, order, or rule," as to _____ with the new regulations.

comply

16. Let your knowledge of English suggest still another variant. If directions are complicated, they are involved or com_____.

com*plex*

17. The color, texture, and general appearance of your skin, particularly of your face, is spoken of as your com_____.

com*plexion*

18. Because the body was originally thought to be a "folding together" of four humors, it was considered complex, hence the word *com*_____.

com*plexion*

19. These next variants are not so frequently found but are still useful shortcuts. With *pli,* change the *i* to *e* as you think of a word describing an individual who is limber and flexible, a sup_____ individual.

sup*ple*

20. This variant helps you define *duple* as meaning

     durable
     stupid
     sensible
     two-fold
     two-faced.

two-fold

21. A flat double "fold" in cloth or other material is called a _____ (rhymes with *eat*), still another variant.

pleat

22. *Plait* is another variant. When you plait some material you

     pleat it
     wear it
     sew it
     weave it.

pleat it

23. Still another variant is found in the word meaning, literally, "to fold apart," or exhibit to advantage as in a show window where goods are placed on dis_____.

dis*play*

24. In addition to *pli, ple,* and *pla,* there is *ploy.* When you use several men to complete a job, probably paying them, you can be said to em_____ them.

em*ploy*

25. And in a military operation, when troops are spread out, we say they are de_____ed.

de*ploy*ed

26. Now you have been introduced to the multi_____ity of forms to be noted for *plicare.*

multi*plic*ity

27. It is quite a step from *multiplicity* to its opposite—freedom from complexity, or sim_____.

sim*plicity*

28. Now you are ready to deal more effectively with the hundreds of words derived from *plicare,* meaning "to _____."

fold

Review Exercise VI

A. In the blank after each root in the left-hand column, write the number, from the right-hand list, of the common meaning of the root. The same meaning may apply to more than one root. Some meanings will not be used at all.

1. *scribere* _____
2. *facere* _____
3. *tendere* _____
4. *specere* _____
5. *plicare* _____

1. speak
2. see
3. write
4. have, hold
5. fold
6. make, do
7. press
8. stretch

B. From each group of words, select the one word whose meaning is most like that of one of the roots in section A. Enter the appropriate letter in the blank at the right.

1. a) scribble, b) scrimmage, c) scrimp, d) sculpture   1. _____
2. a) face, b) manufacture, c) fade, d) failure   2. _____
3. a) tenor, b) tenpins, c) extend, d) tempo   3. _____
4. a) special, b) speedy, c) speech, d) spectator   4. _____
5. a) plod, b) pliant, c) plural, d) plunge   5. _____

Note the phrase in quotation marks in each sentence and express the same idea with a word containing a form of one of the roots in section A.

1. "Write-down" as in the sentence, "Did you read his graphic _____ of the leading character?"
2. "Able-to-be-done" as in the sentence, "His plan was the most_____ of all."
3. "Stretch-to" as in "He will _____ every one of the meetings."
4. "See-into" as in "Do you want to _____ the finished product?"
5. "Fold-in" as in "It was not so much what he said as what he _____ that bothered me."

(Answers on page 253)

Vocabulary Review List

Scribere
describe
scribe
scribble
subscribe
inscribe
transcribe
ascribe
description
descriptive
scripture
script
scrip
scriptorium
scrivener
rescript
proscribe
superscript
prescription
postscript
conscription
circumscribe

Facere
facsimile
facile
facility
fact
factory
benefactor
manufacture
efficacious
artifice
edifice
imperfection
fashionable
feat
feasible

benefit
counterfeit
defect

Tendere
attention
extension
tent
retention
extent
tense
tension
tensile
tendency
tend
intend
intention
superintendent
pretending
pretend
attend
contend
ostentatious
subtend
distend

Specere
spectator
inspect
expect
retrospect
prospect
circumspect
introspection
perspective
respect
aspect

specter
specimen
speculum
specious
spectator
suspect
suspicion
despise
despicable
despicably
auspices
spy
perspicacious

Plicare
complicated
accomplice
pliable
imply
supplicant
implicate
explicate
explicitly
supplicant
plywood
comply
complex
complexion
supple
duple
pleat
plait
display
employ
deploy
multiplicity
simplicity

31   *Stare* ∽

1. The Latin verb *stare* means "to stand." When you drop the *-re,* you have the form common to most English derivatives, the base form _____ .

sta

2. If you like to travel to lands that "stand" far away, you prefer far-off places and di_____ lands.

di*stant*

3. Out on the golf course, when you are about to address the ball, you take your "stand" or, as we more frequently say, your _____ .

stance

4. If a person "stands" firm in purpose and steady in loyalties, we call him con_____ .

con*stant*

5. When a country is given permanent organization—is "stood" on its feet, so to speak—we say it is founded or e____blished.

e*sta*blished

6. When you add *ex-* to *stant,* the *x* already ends in an *s* sound, so you drop the *s* in *stant* to make *ex*_____ , which means "not lost or destroyed," as an old manuscript which still stands or remains out for inspection.

ex*tant*

7. If something "stands" in your way or obstructs progress we call it an ob_____.

obs*tacle*

8. When a man is brought to trial, he is seldom judged on circum_____ evidence only.

circum*stantial*

9. A circumstance is a factor attending an act, event, or condition. Circumstantial evidence is, therefore, evidence surrounding that act—literally "_____ing around (circum-)" it.

*stand*ing

10. Our word *status,* meaning "standing or rank," comes from Latin directly into English without change; it is another principal part of *stare,* meaning "to _____."

stand

11. Dropping the *-us* ending in *status* gives you another important variant form to look for, the form _____.

stat

12. This form is found in many English words. The terminal or "standing" place for trains and buses is called a _____ion.

*stat*ion

13. When a train moves into the station and stops, it is then not moving, or is _____.

stationary

14. A piece of sculpture "standing" on a pedestal is usually spoken of as a _____.

statue

15. If a man is restored to his old position or state, we would say he was rein_____.

rein*stated*

16. Still another variant comes from the related verb form *sistere,* meaning "to cause to stand." Dropping the three-letter sign of the infinitive leaves the base form _____.

sist

17. This form opens up countless other possibilities. If a man demands his rights, "standing" firm "in" those demands, we say he _____ on his rights.

insists

18. If, despite all kinds of opposition, a man continues to press forward on his course, we say he is per_____.

per*sistent*

19. If a man "stands back" in an attempt to elude capture by police officers, we say he is re_____ arrest.

re*sisting*

20. Now think of the prefix that means "to or toward." Add it to *sist* to get the word that means to help someone do something—in other words, to _____ someone.

assist

21. If you take the prefix meaning "together," and add it to a form of *stare,* you get a word meaning "made up of or composed of certain parts"—the word _____.

consist

22. In a few words the root is *sti* or *st* instead of *sta* or *sist,* as in the word describing the stopping or "standing still" of armed hostilities—the word *armi*_____.

armi*stice*

23. The same form is used when talking about the time of year when the sun reaches the farthest point from the equator, north or south—the sol_____.

sol*stice*

24. When something happens to a regular teacher so he is not able to meet his classes, another is sometimes "stood" in his place—a _____ teacher.

substitute

25. If a platform is stable, your knowledge of roots will remind you that it _____ firmly in place.

stands

Review statement

26. Be on the alert from now on for *sta, stat, sti,* and *sist*— all suggesting the meaning "to _____."

stand

32   *Ferre* ∿

1. Take the Latin verb *ferre* and drop the last two letters to get the base form most often found in English, the form _____.

2. Remembering that a common meaning of *re-* is "back," if *refer* means literally "to bear or carry back," you would infer that *ferre* means "to _____ or _____."

3. *Ferre* is an irregular verb with *latus* as one of its forms. Drop the *-us* ending from *latus* to get the other important form in English, the form _____.

4. With *lat,* do not overlook the possibility of a silent *e* to be added, bringing you to an even more common form, as in the English word *re_____*, which means to carry back or tell.

5. In a football or basketball game, the person to whom matters are "carried" or referred for decision is called a re_____.

6. A boat designed to "carry" passengers over a narrow body of water is called a ＿＿＿＿＿＿＿ boat.

ferry

7. A cone-bearing tree is technically known as a coni＿＿＿＿ous tree.

coni*fer*ous

8. In the same way, *pest-bearing* becomes, in a word, *pesti*＿＿＿＿＿＿.

pesti*ferous*

9. Watch out for possible confusion between the Latin noun *ferrum,* meaning "iron," and the Latin verb ＿＿＿＿＿＿, meaning "to bear or carry."

ferre

10. Strangely enough both roots are found in a single word—*ferriferous.* Your root knowledge should help you define a ferriferous rock as an ＿＿＿＿＿-＿＿＿＿＿＿ rock.

iron-bearing

11. As you can see, often an extra letter is inserted between two roots to bring them together into a single word. In *ferriferous* as in *pestiferous* it is the letter ＿.

i

12. Try some word coining of your own. If *vocare* is a Latin verb meaning "to call," the word meaning clamorous or "noise-bearing" would probably be ＿＿＿＿*i*＿＿＿＿＿＿＿.

*voci*ferous

13. This should prepare you nicely for such technical words as *floriferous,* which you would assume to mean

thorn-bearing
leaf-bearing
flower-bearing
fruit-bearing.

flower-bearing

14. And you would infer that *fructiferous* probably means

leaf-bearing
fruit-bearing
thorn-bearing.

fruit-bearing

15. If soil produces abundant crops and is rich in nutrients, it is appropriately spoken of as _____tile.

*fer*tile

16. When two people get together to talk over matters, we say they con_____ about them.

con*fer*

17. If you "carry" into what you read certain things that lie between the lines, you are said to be making in_____.

in*ferences*

18. During a church service a collection or of_____ is usually taken up.

of*fering*

19. If you are literally "borne under" by pain, you are said to suf_____ pain.

suf*fer*

20. If you remember that *dis-* means "apart," when two people are "carried apart" by their conflicting views, we say that they _____.

differ

21. Now for the other basic form, *lat* (or *late*). If you "carry" ideas across from one language to another, it is called trans_____ing.

trans*lat*ing

22. When you speak of something in exaggerated terms, with more enthusiasm than usual, you probably use super_____.

super*latives*

23. Judging from root meaning, when you correlate sets of figures, you probably

    list them
    add them
    compare them.

compare them

24. If you are "carried" out of your usual self by some good news, you are no doubt in a state of e_____ion.

e*lat*ion

25. If you witness an accident and then tell a friend about it, you are said to re_____ the story to him.

re*late*

26. You would infer from your knowledge of prefix and root elements that *illative* probably means

    opinionated
    inferential
    wishful
    exhausting.

inferential

27. And a prolate spheroid is probably a spheroid that is

    elongated
    irregular
    small.

elongated
(or "carried" out)

Review statement

28. Now whenever you spot a word with either *fer* or *lat* you will know to look for the meaning or idea, "to bear or _____."

carry

33   *Graphein* ~

1. In the Latin verb *tenere,* the last three letters indicate the infinitive. In the Greek verb *graphein,* the last three letters also indicate the _____.

infinitive

2. *Graphein* is in the infinitive form. Does it mean "I write" or "to write"?

to write

3. As is the case with most Latin verbs, that part of *graphein* which most frequently comes over into English is found by dropping the infinitive ending to get the form _____.

graph

4. A diagram representing changes by means of a curve or series of bars is spoken of as a _____.

graph

5. A host of words are made through suffix additions. For example, the substance in a pencil that does the "writing" is called _____ite.

*graph*ite

6. And if you give us a realistic, vivid description of a scene, it can appropriately be called a graph_____ description.

graph*ic*

7. If a monolith is, literally, a "single stone," a "writer in stone" or one who prints from stone plates would be called a litho_____.

litho*grapher*

8. Just as the letter *i* connects *pest* and *ferous* in *pestiferous,* so when adding *lith* to *grapher* we need a letter to make the two parts sound like one word. In this case the connecting letter is the letter __.

o

9. It is possible, in a sense, to "write with light." Using a camera it is possible to take a picture or photo_____ something.

photo*graph*

10. Knowing that *photography* is "light-writing" you can infer that the combining form *photo-* means "_____."

light

11. In this day and age, to "write with sound" is also possible. We can buy records with "sound-writing" and play them on our own phono_____.

phono*graph*

12. Now you should be able to infer that *phono-* means "_____."

sound

13. Famous people are often plagued by people who want them to sign or _____ their names.

autograph

14. If *ortho-* is from a Greek word meaning "straight," writing or spelling words in a correct fashion is the science or subject _____ (rhymes with *geography*).

orthography

15. You might expect the writing of prostitutes to be obscene. If you know that the Greek word, *porne,* means "prostitute," you know where we got our word porno_____.

porno*graphy*

16. If our word *lexicon* means "dictionary," you would expect the "writer" of a dictionary to be a lexico_____.

lexico*grapher*

17. If a pyromaniac is one with a persistent compulsion to start destructive fires, one skilled in burning designs on wood or leather would be a p_____.

p*yrographer*

18. If the combining form *seismo* means "earthquake," then an instrument for recording or writing earthquake shocks would be a _____.

seismograph

19. In printing, a person skilled in setting, arranging, or writing with type is not called a type grapher but, in a word, a _____.

typographer

20. If you know that *topos* is a Greek word meaning "place," a survey of some place with all its contours represented would be called a _____ical survey.

*topographi*cal

21. If *chiro-* is a combining form meaning "hand," an expert penman or handwriter would be a _____.

chirographer

22. If you know that *steno-* means "narrow," you can see why one who records in a narrow space (by shorthand) what is said is called a _____.

stenographer

23. The Greek word *mimos* means "imitator," which suggests why a machine for making imitations or copies of written material is called a _____ machine.

mimeograph

24. If the Greek word *chorein* means "choral dance," the person who designs the movements of a ballet would be the _____.

choreographer

25. Knowledge of English should lead you to the only important variant form of *graph*. A telegraph message is called a tele_____.

tele*gram*

26. In school when you study a language, you usually study the rules for its use or its writing—in other words, its _____.

grammar

Review statement

27. In reviewing this unit, remember the two most com-
    mon forms of *graphein* are _____ and
    _____, meaning "to _____."

graph, gram
write

34   *Logos* ∾

1. What is the best way to remember the three key meanings of the Greek noun *logos*? Try mnemonics as your aid to m_____.

memory

2. Let us start with the original meaning of *logos*— "speech or word." Associate this meaning with the word *monologue,* one person making a "speech" or saying _____.

words

3. Another meaning is "reason." To remember this more easily, think of the word suggesting the use of correct reasoning, our word _____*ic*.

logic

4. It is a short step from "reason" to "science of" or "study of," as in geo_____, the study of individual rock types.

geology

5. For a closer look at variant forms, drop the *s* from *logos* to get the form _____, as found in *logograph,* meaning a kind of word puzzle.

logo

6. Now drop the *o* from *logo* to get the even shorter form _____, as in *monolog*.

log

7. Another, longer spelling of *monolog* brings you to still another variant, the form _____, as in *monologue*.

logue

8. And in many words the form is *logy,* as in the science of bio_____.

bio*logy*

9. Knowing the forms *logo, log, logue,* and *logy,* you should now be able to identify the more than 150 English words derived from the Greek noun _____.

logos

10. If *philein* is a Greek word meaning "love," a "word-lover" or "student of words" is appropriately called a philo_____ist.

philo*log*ist

11. The Greek word *astron* means "star." The so-called "science of" the stars, foretelling their influence on human affairs, is astro_____.

astro*logy*

12. Going a step farther, if the Greek word *nautes* means "sailor," a "sailor" or navigator in the "stars" would be rightly called an astro_____.

astro*naut*

13. Introductory lines or verses in a play or poem would be called a pro_____.

pro*logue*

14. If the word *decade* means a group of "ten," the Ten Commandments or ten "words" would be called the _____logue.

*deca*logue

15. Two people talking together, as in a play, will give us a dia_____.

dia*logue*

16. A "study of" myths would appropriately be called m_____.

m*ythology*

17. And "words" about travel give us the handy word t_____.

t*ravelogue*

18. The Greek word *etymon* refers to the literal sense of a word. The "study of" the origin and development of words would, therefore, be called *etymo*_____.

etymo*logy*

19. If a euphonious sound is good to listen to, a "speech" of praise would be called a eu_____.

eu*logy*

20. The "study of" crime is known as _____.

criminology

21. In every field there is a special nomenclature that must be mastered—the various technical terms in the field. This is spoken of as the t_____inology.

ter*m*inology

22. When you speak of life as being like a river, that type of comparison is called an ana_____.

ana*logy*

23. If *kata* is a Greek word meaning "down or completely," a complete "writing" down of all items for sale, as for a mail order house, would be called a _____log.

*cata*log

24. Thinking in terms of the original meaning of logos, you would expect the word *tetralogy* to refer to a series of four

    buildings
    pictures
    dramas
    pantomimes.

dramas

25. Judging from the original meaning, *tautology* is apparently a word relating to

    customs
    phrases
    desires
    foods.

phrases

26. A neologism would apparently be a new

    conclusion
    word
    amount
    task.

word

27. The noun *logos* comes from the verb *legein*, "to speak," hence the forms *lex* and *lect* as in such words as _____icon and *dia*_____.

*lex*icon
dia*lect*

Review statement

28. In addition to the meanings "speech" and "words," the other two meanings of *logos* to remember are "reason" and "_____ of."

science

Review Exercise VII

A. In the blank after each root in the left-hand column, write the number, from the right-hand list, of the common meaning of the root. The same meaning may apply to more than one root. Some meanings will not be used at all.

1. *stare*	_____	1. discover
		2. calculate
2. *ferre*	_____	3. stand
		4. see
		5. write
3. *graphein*	_____	6. speech, study of
		7. bear, carry
4. *logos*	_____	8. lower

B. From each group of words, select the one word whose meaning is most like that of one of the roots in section A. Enter the appropriate letter in the blank at the right.

1. a) stalk, b) stable, c) stagger, d) star   1. _____
2. a) ferry, b) ferocious, c) festival, d) fever   2. _____
3. a) grasp, b) grape, c) grapple, d) graph   3. _____
4. a) log, b) logical, c) long, d) lotion   4. _____

C. Note the word or phrase in quotation marks in each sentence and express the same idea with a word containing a form of one of the roots in section A.

1. "Standing" as in the sentence, "He was quite conscious of anything that might affect his _____ in the community."
2. "Carry-in" as in the sentence, "He didn't say so exactly, but I _____ that's what he meant."
3. "Self-written" as in the sentence, "I got him to _____ his latest book."
4. "Speaking-between" as in the sentence, "The _____ in that play is very witty."

(*Answers on page 253*)

Vocabulary Review List

Stare
distant
stance
constant
establish
extant
obstacle
circumstantial
status
station
stationary
statue
reinstate
insist
persistent
resisting
assist
consist
armistice
solstice
substitute
stable

Ferre
relate
refer
referee
ferry
coniferous
pestiferous
ferriferous
pestiferous
vociferous

floriferous
fructiferous
fertile
confer
inference
offering
suffer
differ
translate
superlative
correlate
elation
relate
illative
prolate

Graphein
graph
graphite
graphic
lithographer
photograph
photography
phonograph
autograph
orthography
pornography
lexicographer
pyrographer
seismograph
typographer
topographical
chirographer

stenographer
mimeograph
choreographer
telegram
grammar

Logos
monologue
logic
geology
logograph
monolog
monologue
biology
philologist
astrology
prologue
decalogue
dialogue
mythology
travelogue
etymology
eulogy
criminology
terminology
analogy
catalog
tetralogy
tautology
neologism
lexicon
dialect

Review Essay (continued)

As a review of both prefix and root elements studied so far, fill in the blanks with the appropriate prefixes. As in the earlier portion of the essay, prefix meanings are given in the margin. This provides a desirable reinforcement of the connection between prefix form and meaning.

The review of the roots is handled in a slightly different fashion. Whenever you *perceive a line marked with an asterisk, you know it contains a word with one of the fourteen roots studied. Using your dictionary, check until you find the exact word *with one of those roots. This should serve as a graphic reminder of the role of the *dictionary in verifying your hypotheses about derivation. Furthermore the logic leading to more accurate generalizations should be an important additional outgrowth of Huxley's article. (In the lines above which are marked with an asterisk, you should have discovered *capere* in *perceive*, *graphein* in *graphic*, and *logos* in *logic*.) Now go ahead with your review.

All Men Are Scientists

Thomas Henry Huxley

. . . . So much, then, by way of proof that the
*method of establishing laws in science is exactly the
same as that pursued in common life. Let us now
turn to another matter (though really it is but another phase of the same question), and that is, the
*method by which, from the ___lations of certain   back, again
phenomena, we prove that some stand in the
position of causes towards the others.

I want to put the case clearly before you, and
I will therefore show you what I mean by an-
*other familiar ___ample. I will ___pose that one   out/under
of you, on coming down in the morning to the
parlour of your house, finds that a tea-pot and
some spoons which had been left in the room on
the ___vious evening are gone,—the window   before
is open, and you ___serve the mark of a dirty   against
hand on the window-frame, and ___haps, in   through
___dition to that, you notice the ___press of a   to/into
hob-nailed shoe on the gravel outside. All these
*phenomena have struck your ___tention ___-   to/into
*stantly, and before two seconds have passed you
say, "Oh, somebody has broken open the window,
___tered the room, and run off with the spoons   in

out

out

and the tea-pot!" That speech is out of your mouth in a moment. And you will probably add, "I know there has; I am quite sure of it!" You mean to say ___actly what you know; but in reality you are giving ___pression to what is, in all essential particulars, an hypothesis. You do not *know* it at all; it is nothing but an hypothesis rapidly framed in your own mind. And it is an *hypothesis founded on a long train of inductions and deductions.

against

into

together

to or toward

back, again

before

out

forward

before

apart

together

What are those inductions and deductions, and how have you got at this hypothesis? You have ___served, in the first place, that the window is open; but by a train of reasoning ___volving many inductions and deductions, you have probably arrived long before at the general law—and a very good one it is—that windows do not open of themselves; and you therefore ___clude that something has opened the window. A second general law that you have ___rived at in the same way is, that tea-pots and spoons do not go out of a window spontaneously, and you are satisfied that, as they are not now where you left them, they have been ___moved. In the third place, you look at the marks on the window-sill, and the shoe-marks outside, and you say that in all___-vious ___perience the former kind of mark has never been ___duced by anything else but the hand of a human being; and the same experience shows that no other animal but man at ___sent wears shoes with hob-nails in them such as would *produce the marks in the gravel. I do not know, even if we could ___cover any of those "missing links" that are talked about, that they would help us to any other ___clusion! At any rate the law which states our present experience is strong *enough for my present purpose. You next reach the conclusion, that as these kinds of marks have not been left by any other animals than men, or are liable to be formed in any other way than by a man's hand and shoe, the marks in question have been formed by a man in that way. You

have, further, a general law, founded on __serva-
tion and experience, and that, too, is, I am sorry
to say, a very universal and _____peachable one,
—that some men are thieves; and you __sume at
*once from all these _____mises—and that is what
_____stitutes your hypothesis—that the man who
made the marks outside and on the window-sill,
opened the window, got into the room, and stole
your tea-pot and spoons. You have now arrived
at a *vera causa;*—you have __sumed a cause
*which, it is plain, is _____petent to produce all the
phenomena you have __served. You can __plain
all these phenomena only by the hypothesis of a
thief. But that is a hypothetical conclusion, of the
justice of which you have no __solute proof at
all; it is only rendered highly _____bable by a
series of inductive and deductive reasonings.

I suppose your first action, __suming that you
are a man of ordinary common sense, and that
you have established this hypothesis to your own
satisfaction, will very likely be to go for the police,
and set them on the track of the burglar, with the
view to the __covery of your property. But just
as you are starting with this __ject, some person
comes in, and on learning what you are about,
says, "My good friend, you are going on a great
deal too fast. How do you know that the man who
really made the marks took the spoons? It might
have been a monkey that took them, and the man
may have merely looked in afterwards." You
*would probably __ply, "Well, that is all very
well, but you see it is contrary to all experience
of the way tea-pots and spoons are __stracted; so
that, at any rate, your hypothesis is less probable
than mine." While you are talking the thing over
in this way, another friend __rives. And he might
say, "Oh, my dear sir, you are certainly going on
a great deal too fast. You are most _____sumptu-
*ous. You __mit that all these __currences took
place when you were fast asleep, at a time when
you could not possibly have known anything
about what was taking place. How do you know

against

not/not
to
before
together, with

to
together
against/out

away
forward, for

to

back, again
against

back, again

away

to

before
to/against

that the laws of nature are not____pended dur-   under
ing the night? It may be that there has been some
*kind of supernatural _____ference in this   between
case." In point of fact, he __clares that your   down, away
hypothesis is one of which you cannot at all
__monstrate the truth and that you are by no   down, away
means sure that the laws of Nature are the same
when you are asleep as when you are awake.

Well, now, you cannot at the moment answer
that kind of reasoning. You feel that your worthy
friend has you somewhat at a _____vantage.   not/to
*You will feel ____fectly ____vinced in your own   through/with
mind, however, that you are quite right, and you
say to him, "My good friend, I can only be guided
by the natural ____babilities of the case, and if   forward, for
you will be kind enough to stand aside and
____mit me to pass, I will go and fetch the po-   through
lice." Well, we will suppose that your journey is
____cessful, and that by good luck you meet   under
with a policeman; that __ventually the burglar is   out
found with your property on his person, and the
marks _____spond to his hand and to his   together, with/back, again
boots. Probably any jury would ____sider those   together, with
*facts a very good experimental verification of your
hypothesis, touching the cause of the __normal   away
phenomena __served in your parlour, and would   against
act __cordingly.   to
* Now, in this _____positious case, I have taken   under
phenomena of a very common kind, in order that
*you might see what are the different steps in an
ordinary _____cess of reasoning, if you will only   for
take the trouble to analyze it carefully. All the
*operations I have __scribed, you will see, are   down
__volved in the mind of any man of sense in   into
leading him to a conclusion as to the course he
should take in order to make good a robbery and
punish the __fender. I say that you are led, in   against
that case, to your conclusion by exactly the same
train of reasoning as that which a man of science
pursues when he is __deavouring to _____cover   in/apart
the origin and laws of the most __cult phenom-   against
ena. The process is, and always must be, the

before
in, into
down, away

down/apart
in
away

to
with

into
with/forward
wrong/back, again
to, toward/wrong
not

back

into/to

under

down, away/to, toward
under/to, toward
distant
against/down, away
together, with

apart

together

same; and ___cisely the same mode of reason-
*ing was ___ployed by Newton and Laplace in
their endeavours to discover and ___fine the
causes of the movements of the heavenly bodies,
as you, with your own common sense, would employ to ___tect a burglar. The only ___ference
is, that the nature of the ___quiry being more
___struse, every step has to be most carefully
watched, so that there may not be a single crack
or flaw in your hypothesis. A flaw or crack in
many of the hypotheses of daily life may be
*of little or no moment as ___fecting the general
___rectness of the conclusions at which we may
arrive; but, in a scientific inquiry, a fallacy, great
or small, is always of ___portance, and is sure to
*be in the long run ___stantly ___ductive of
___chievous, if not fatal ___sults.

Do not ___low yourselves to be ___led by the
common notion that an hypothesis is ___trust-
worthy simply because it is an hypothesis. It is
*often urged, in ___spect to some scientific con-
clusion, that, after all, it is only an hypothesis. But
what more have we to guide us in nine-tenths of
*the most ___portant ___fairs of daily life than
hypotheses, and often very ill-based ones? So that
in science, where the evidence of any hypothesis
is ___jected to the most rigid examination, we
may rightly pursue the same course. You may
have hypotheses and hypotheses. A man may say,
if he likes, that the moon is made of green cheese:
that is an hypothesis. But another man, who has
*___voted a great deal of time and ___tention to
the ___ject, and ___vailed himself of the most
powerful ___scopes and the results of the
___servations of others, ___clares that in his
*opinion it is probably ___posed of materials
very similar to those of which our own earth is
made up: and that is also only an hypothesis. But
I need not tell you that there is an enormous
___ference in the value of the two hypotheses.
That one which is based on sound scientific
knowledge is sure to have a ___responding

forward/apart

down, away/against

against

against/to

not/out

for

together

to

with

back, again/down, away

into/to

value; and that which is a mere hasty random guess is likely to have but little value. Every great step in our _____gress in _____covering causes has been made in exactly the same way as that which I have __tailed to you. A person __serving the *__currences of certain facts and phenomena asks, naturally enough, what process, what kind *of operation known to __cur in Nature __plied to the particular case, will __ravel and __plain the mystery? Hence you have the scientific hypothesis and its value will be _____portionate to the care and _____pleteness with which its basis has been tested and verified. It is in these matters *as in the commonest __fairs of practical life: the guess of the fool will be folly, while the guess of *the wise man will _____tain wisdom. In all cases, you see that the value of the __sult __pends on the patience and faithfulness with which the *__vestigator __plies to his hypothesis every kind of verification. . . .

Part IV Suffixes

Suffixes

Suffixes provide a natural complement to any study of prefix and root elements. For example, the word *compose* is now easily broken into its respective parts— *com-,* meaning "together," and *pose,* from *ponere,* meaning "to put or place." When you compose a letter, you literally put the words together that make it a letter. It is at this point that suffixes enter the picture, providing further modifications of that basic meaning.

1. When you talk about one who composes, you are talking about a compos_____.

-er

2. When you put separate parts or elements together to make something, what you have made is properly called a compos_____ of those elements.

-ite

3. That which is so formed by a putting together of parts is called a compos_____.

-ition

4. A typesetter is also known as a compos_____.

-itor

In exploring the role of suffixes, suppose you first read the meaning of each of the suffixes given below. Then think of a word to enter after each suffix in the blank at the right.

Suffixes	Meanings	Words with Suffixes
	I	
-able	Capable or worthy of the expressed or implied verb action	_____
-er	one who or something that performs the action indicated by the root form	_____
-al	pertinence to or connection with	_____
-cule	smallness	_____
-tion	an action or process	_____
	II	
-ent	having attendency or inclination to perform an act	_____
-esque	used to form adjectives which have the quality of the main word element	_____
-ess	a female	_____
-ile	relationship with similarity to or capability of	_____
-hood	state, condition, or quality of being	_____
	III	
-ate	to cause to	_____
-dom	condition or state	_____
-ish	resembling	_____
-less	without	_____
-ward	in the direction of	_____

Suffixes	Meanings	Words with Suffixes
	IV	
-ock	a diminutive	_____
-ory	having the nature of	_____
-ose	full of	_____
-ster	one who	_____
-trix	feminine ending	_____

Succinctness Through Suffixes

Suffixes are particularly useful in letting you express an idea with admirable conciseness, as in the examples given below. For each of the phrases, use a suffix to say the same thing with one word only.

1. A small hill or mound is a hill_____.

-ock

2. The state of being wise is what is called wis_____.

-dom

3. Of or pertaining to an infant is infant_____.

-ile

4. Full of or characterized by fraud is fraud_____.

-ulent

5. One who is young is youth_____.

-ful

6. A woman aviator is an avia_____.

-trix

7. Something capable of being retracted is retract_____.

-able

8. If someone works without tiring, he is tire_____.

-less

9. If it is a situation which lends itself to remedy, it is remedi_____.

-al

10. If it is in the manner or style of a picture, it can be called pictur_____.

-esque

11. One who helps is a help_____.

-er

12. To cause something to become antique is to antiqu_____ it.

-ate

13. A female lion is a lion_____.

-ess

14. Something resembling a book is book_____.

-ish

15. A minute globe is a glob_____.

-ule

16. Having the nature of a commendation means it is commendat_____.

-ory

17. The act of instigating a move is an instiga_____.

-tion

18. A scheme that is full of grandeur is rightly called grandi_____.

-ose

19. If the action tends toward a conclusion, it is conclus_____.

-ive

20. If the object moved in the direction of heaven it moved in a heaven_____ direction.

-ly

Changing Parts of Speech

Using the appropriate suffixes, turn the following words into adjectives. Try to avoid using any *-ing* or *-ed* endings. Cover the answers in the margin with a 3 x 5 card and go through the list as rapidly as possible.

1. advise

   advisable (or advisory)

2. earth

   earthen (or earthly)

3. glory

   glorious

4. please

   pleasant (or pleasing)

5. quarrel

   quarrelsome (or quarreling)

6. mess

   messy (or messed)

7. tiger

   tigerlike (or tigerish)

8. profit

   profitable

9. nation

   national

10. erupt

   eruptive (or erupting)

Turn the following words into verbs, through the addition of appropriate suffixes. For example, turn *glad* into *gladden* with an *-en* and the corresponding change of spelling.

1. active

   activate

2. soft

   soften

3. sterile

   sterilize

4. solid

   solidify

5. coalescence

   coalesce

6. example

   exemplify

7. refrigerator

   refrigerate

8. dark

   darken

9. machine

   mechanize

10. mature

   matured

Turn the following words into agent nouns—someone or something acting or doing something. For example, you could turn piano into someone playing the piano by adding *-ist*.

1. assess

    assessor

2. music

    musician

3. motor

    motorist

4. engine

    engineer

5. intoxicate

    intoxicant

6. poem

    poet or poetess

7. brag

    braggart or bragger

8. spin

    spinner or spinster

9. cool

    cooler

10. employ

    employee or employer

Turn the following words into abstract nouns, words meaning a state, act, or condition. For example, turn *apply* into *application*.

1. advertise

    advertisement

2. depart

    departure

3. sweet

    sweetness

4. loyal

    loyalty

5. man

    manhood

6. baptize

    baptism

7. admit

    admission

8. approve

    approval

9. brave

    bravery

10. jealous

    jealousy or jealousness

Two-Stage Review

I. *Difficult Stage:* In the following news stories, underline *all* prefix and root elements that you recognize as having studied. See how close you can come to discovering all such elements present.

UNION PROPOSALS TO GO TO CONGRESS CABINET—"D" Head

Proposed plans for improvement of facilities in the Union will be released Tuesday to the president's cabinet of all-University congress. It will then be reviewed by all student organizations on campus and eventually by the senate committee on student affairs.

The proposal, result of an extensive survey made by a University committee under the chairmanship of Dr. Theodore Taplow, associate professor of sociology, deals mainly with rearrangement of the Union ground floor to better accommodate the commuters' lunchroom.

The report suggested moving the lunchroom from the basement to the space now occupied by the Union book store and postoffice, leaving only general delivery mail service and completely dropping the postoffice box system of campus mail.

Starting with the premise that (1) "the commuters' lunchroom is horrible and (2) that something has to be done about it," the committee presented this proposal as their solution to the problem.

However, the proposal is not offered as a permanent solution. It is a suggestion for rearrangement of present facilities to better advantage. Sometime in the next decade it will probably be necessary to add space to the building by construction of a new wing, excavation of the unfinished sub-basement area or roofing over one floor of the terrace.

TCRT Announces 20-Cent Cash Rate For Commuters

The fare for inter-city commuters to the University under the TCRT reduced fare experiment will be 20 cents cash or one token plus two cents cash, Luther Bakken, company general superintendent of transportation, said yesterday.

Last week TCRT released information that the single fare would be 20 cents cash or one token during November and December. Bakken said this move had not been approved at the time by the state railroad and warehouse commission.

The commission last week approved the special fare, but did not say what the fare would be. Bakken expects the commission to set the fare at 20 cents cash next week.

(From *The Minnesota Daily*)

II. *Easier Stage:* Here are the same two stories. This time you have specific clues as to how many elements are in each line. The number of blanks under the headings *prefixes* and *roots* will indicate the number of elements present in each line. Enter the infinitive form of the verbs and the common form of the prefixes. Check the answers when you finish and compare your scores with the more difficult stage that you did earlier.

PREFIXES   ROOTS

			UNION PROPOSALS TO GO	
1. ___			TO CONGRESS CABINET	1. ___
2. ___			Proposed plans for improvement	
3. ___	4. ___		of facilities in the Union will	2. ___
			be released Tuesday to the	3. ___
5. ___			president's cabinet of all-Uni-	
6. ___			versity congress. It will then be	
7. ___			reviewed by all student organizations	
8. ___			on campus and eventually by the	
9. ___			senate committee on student	4. ___
10. ___			affairs	5. ___
11. ___			The proposal, result of an	6. ___
12. ___	13. ___		extensive survey made by a University	7. ___
14. ___			committee under the chairmanship of	8. ___
15. ___			Dr. Taplow, associate professor of	
16. ___	17. ___		sociology, deals mainly with rear-	
18. ___	19. ___		rangement of the Union ground floor	
20. ___	21. ___	22. ___	to better accommodate the commuters'	
			lunchroom.	
23. ___	24. ___		The report suggested moving the	
			lunchroom from the basement to the	
25. ___			space now occupied by the Union book	
			store and postoffice, leaving	9. ___
26. ___			only general delivery mail service	
27. ___			and completely dropping the post-	
			office box system of campus mail.	10. ___
28. ___			Starting with the premise that	11. ___
29. ___			(1) "the commuters' lunchroom is	
			horrible and (2) that something	
			has to be done about it," the	
30. ___	31. ___		committee presented this	12. ___
32. ___			proposal as their solution to	13. ___
33. ___			the problem.	
34. ___			However, the proposal is not	
35. ___	36. ___		offered as a permanent solution.	14. ___
37. ___	38. ___	39. ___	It is a suggestion for rearrange-	15. ___
40. ___			ment of present facilities to	
41. ___			better advantage. Sometime in the	16. ___
42. ___			next decade it will probably	
			be necessary to add space to the	
43. ___			building by construction of a new	
44. ___	45. ___		wing, excavation of the unfinished	
46. ___			subbasement area or roofing over	
			one floor of the terrace.	

Answers: PREFIXES—1. *pro-,* 2. *com-,* 3. *pro-,* 4. *in-,* 5. *re-,* 6. *pre-,* 7. *com-,* 8. *re-,* 9. *ex-,* 10. *com-,* 11. *ad-,* 12. *pro-,* 13. *re-,* 14. *ex-,* 15. *com-,* 16. *ad-,* 17. *pro-,* 18. *re-,* 19. *ad-,* 20. *ad-,* 21. *com-,* 22. *com-,* 23. *re-,* 24. *sub-,* 25. *ob-,* 26. *de-,* 27. *com-,* 28. *pre-,* 29. *com-,* 30. *com-,* 31. *pre-,* 32. *pro-,* 33. *pro-,* 34. *pro-,* 35. *ob-,* 36. *per-,* 37. *sub-,* 38. *re-,* 39. *ad-,* 40. *pre-,* 41. *ad-,* 42. *pro-,* 43. *com-,* 44. *ex-,* 45. *un-,* 46. *sub-.*
ROOTS: 1. *ponere,* 2. *ponere,* 3. *facere,* 4. *mittere,* 5. *facere,* 6. *ponere,* 7. *tenere,* 8. *mittere,* 9. *facere,* 10. *facere,* 11. *mittere,* 12. *mittere,* 13. *ponere,* 14. *ponere,* 15. *ferre,* 16. *facere.*

III. Here is another short article taken from the same source. Do it in the same way.

PREFIXES   ROOTS

1. _____
2. _____   *TCRT Announces 20-Cent*
3. _____   *Cash Rate for Commuters*
4. _____   The fare for inter-city
5. _____   6. _____   commuters to the University under the   1. _____
                     TCRT reduced fare experiment will be
                     20 cents cash or one token plus two
7. _____   cents cash, Luther Bakken, company gen-
8. _____   9. _____   eral superintendent of transportation,   2. _____
                     said yesterday.
10. _____ 11. _____   Last week TCRT released information
                     that the single fare would be 20 cents
                     cash or one token during November
                     and December.
                     Bakken said this move had not been
12. _____   approved at the time by the state   3. _____
13. _____   railroad and warehouse commission.   4. _____
14. _____ 15. _____   The commission last week approved   5. _____
                     the special fare, but did not say what
16. _____   the fare would be. Bakken expects the   6. _____
17. _____   commission to set the fare at 20 cents   7. _____
                     cash next week.

Answers: PREFIXES—1. *ad-,* 2. *com-,* 3. *inter-,* 4. *com-,* 5. *re-,* 6. *ex-,* 7. *com-,* 8. *in-,* 9. *trans-,* 10. *re-,* 11. *in-,* 12. *ad-,* 13. *com-,* 14. *com-,* 15. *ad-,* 16. *ex-,* 17. *com-.*
ROOTS: 1. *ducere,* 2. *tendere,* 3. *stare,* 4. *mittere,* 5. *mittere,* 6. *specere,* 7. *mittere.*

Extending Your Gains

At this point what can you do to insure that your study of these few all-important elements will make the maximum contribution to your handling of all other prefix, root, and suffix items—the thousand you have not studied here? You need the following three steps:

1) Look for one of the 34 prefix or root elements or for one of the suffixes studied.

2) If you find one, think of its common meaning. If you do not find one, you must arrive at a hypothetical common meaning by listing several words beginning with the same letters as the unknown element, defining each word that you list. You then determine what meaning is common to all the words listed, which should bring you as close as possible to the meaning of the unknown element.

3) Finally, check general contextual clues to corroborate or modify your hypothesis about word meaning arrived at through attention to word parts, a derivational context, so to speak.

Let's see how this works. Suppose, for example, you are taking a civil service examination. In the vocabulary test you come to the strange word *omnitude,* in the test item:

omnitude—1) honor, 2) allness, 3) attitude, 4) deafness, 5) solitude

The natural reaction when coming to a perfectly strange word is to say to yourself, *"Omnitude!* I never heard of that word. I guess I'll have to skip that item and go on to the next."

You have the advantage over others, however, since you know the three key steps to make. Try those steps now.

1) Look for a familiar element. The word does *not* contain one of the 34 elements studied.

2) You now list several words you can think of that begin with *omni-,* the unknown element, defining each briefly.

    List: Common meaning:

   1. omni*present* = always present
   2. omni*potent* = all powerful
   3. omni*vorous* = eating all kinds of food   *all*
   4. omni*scient* = all-knowing

3) In this case, your contextual clues are limited to the choices given in the test item, one of which does corroborate your hypothesis and lead you to the right answer—allness.

When you use these steps, even a strange Latin word may succumb to your analysis and yield its meaning. Take the Latin verb *vocare*. By now, you know enough to drop off the infinitive ending to get the most likely combination to be found in words, the *voc*. List as many words as you can think of with a *voc*, remembering to add prefixes on the front end as well as suffixes to the other end. This will insure that you get *convocation* as well as *vocation, vocal* as well as *vocalize*. After you have listed as many words as possible, you should be very close to the literal meaning of vocare—"to call."

Remember—use those three steps to speed the dynamic continued growth of word power.

Additional Aids

After completing this text, many readers will wish to continue their efforts toward improved word power. Certain aids are particularly useful supplements to the approach taken in this text and are listed below.

Word Parts: Word Power Game. KTCA-TV, Channel 2, 1640 Como Avenue, St. Paul, Minnesota 55108—$2.00 postpaid. Using color-cuing to emphasize prefix, root, and suffix elements, a total of 70 cards, with suggested games to be played, including a vocabulary-building game of solitaire. Since word parts are in a sense almost invisible, these cards make the parts stand out. For example, one root card with the Latin verb *videre* can be used together with twenty other cards in the deck to make over fifty different words. Try listing fifty words with a *vid* and you can see the advantage of using the cards.

Context: Word Clues. Educational Developmental Laboratories, Huntington, New York—$2.20. This provides a programed coverage of 300 words with attention to both dictionary and context as a means of building mastery.

Dictionary: Harbrace Guide to Dictionaries, by Wilson, Hendrickson, and Taylor. Harcourt, Brace and World, Inc., New York—$2.50. Contains 29 selections about the dictionary, focused on what a dictionary is, what kinds there are, and what information is available.

Individualized

Vocabulary-Building Pattern

No specific list of general or technical words is of equal importance to all readers. One reader may not know a single word on such a list, another may know every one, and still a third may know only half of them. Furthermore, technical words in one reader's major field of interest are of particular importance. Of necessity they must be mastered. For another whose major interest is in another field, those same words are of incidental interest and importance. For those reasons no specific list of words to be mastered is given in this text.

Instead space is so structured in the following pages to start you toward mastery of those words which are for you most relevant, no matter what your major field or fields of interest or present level of vocabulary development.

You are to find one example under each of the prefix and root elements studied for entry here. When you have done so you will have gone far toward establishing habits which should insure maximum continued growth of vocabulary. It is an easy matter to use this same pattern to make a vocabulary section for each subject you take as well as for general vocabulary development.

To see how to use these pages to best advantage, look at this sample analysis of the word *effectors*.

Word	*Meaning*	*Context*
(with part of speech and pronunciation) effectors (n) (i · fek′ tərz)	(literal and actual) *ex-* (out) + *facere* (make) organs, as muscles or glands, serving to transform efferent nerve impulses into physical action.	"The nervous system is made up of billions of tiny cells which connect with receptors, effectors, or other nerve cells." (Psych.)

1. Over-   2. Pre-   3. De-   4. Mono-   5. Inter-

Word	*Meaning*	*Context*

1. (Over-) _____

2. (Pre-) _____

3. (De-) _____

4. (Mono-) _____

5. (Inter-) _____

6. Un- 7. Re- 8. Trans- 9. Pro- 10. Non-

	Word	*Meaning*	*Context*

6. (Un-) ——————————

7. (Re-) ——————————

8. (Trans-) ——————————

9. (Pro-) ——————————

10. (Non-) ——————————

11. Epi- 12. Mis- 13. Ob- 14. Ex- 15. Dis-

Word	*Meaning*	*Context*

11. (Epi-) ——————————

12. (Mis-) ——————————

13. (Ob-) ——————————

14. (Ex-) ——————————

15. (Dis-) ——————————

16. In- 17. Com- 18. Sub- 19. In- 20. Ad-

Word	*Meaning*	*Context*

16. (In-) _____

17. (Com-) _____

18. (Sub-) _____

19. (In-) _____

20. (Ad-) _____

21. *Capere*   22. *Ponere*   23. *Tenere*   24. *Ducere*   25. *Mittere*

Word	*Meaning*	*Context*

21. (Capere) _____

22. (Ponere) _____

23. (Tenere) _____

24. (Ducere) _____

25. (Mittere) _____

26. *Scribere* 27. *Facere* 28. *Tendere* 29. *Specere* 30. *Plicare*

Word	*Meaning*	*Context*

26. (Scribere) _____

27. (Facere) _____

28. (Tendere) _____

29. (Specere) _____

30. (Plicare) _____

31. *Stare* 32. *Ferre* 33. *Graphein* 34. *Logos*

Word	*Meaning*	*Context*

31. (Stare) ———————————

32. (Ferre) ———————————

33. (Graphein) ———————————

34. (Logos) ———————————

Answers for the four diagnostic tests:

Test A:	Test B:	Test C:	Test D:
1.3	1.3	1.1	1.5
2.4	2.4	2.4	2.5
3.4	3.4	3.5	3.4
4.1	4.4	4.4	4.1
5.4	5.1	5.1	5.1
6.3	6.5	6.5	6.2
7.2	7.4	7.3	7.5
8.4	8.1	8.4	8.1
9.4	9.2	9.2	9.2
10.5	10.3	10.2	10.5
11.1	11.5	11.1	11.3
12.5	12.1	12.4	12.5
13.1	13.5	13.5	13.3
14.3	14.2	14.1	14.1
15.4	15.2	15.2	15.2
16.1	16.2	16.4	16.4
17.1	17.1	17.2	17.2
18.1	18.4	18.2	18.1
19.3	19.1	19.2	19.4
20.5	20.4	20.3	20.1

ANSWERS:

Test (page 3)

1. 2	6. 1
2. 4	7. 3
3. 5	8. 1
4. 1	9. 5
5. 2	10. 4

The Twenty Prefixes
(page 17)

1. before
2. down, away
3. between, among
4. against, to, toward
5. in, into, not
6. one, alone
7. upon, on, over
8. to, towards
9. not
10. together, with
11. not
12. out, beyond, formerly
13. back, again
14. forward, for
15. not, in, into
16. apart, not
17. above, beyond
18. under, below
19. wrong, wrongly
20. across, beyond

Test—The Fourteen Roots
(page 17)

1. take, seize
2. have, hold
3. send
4. bear, carry
5. stand
6. write
7. speech, word, study
   of, reason
8. see
9. fold, weave
10. stretch
11. lead
12. put, place
13. make, do
14. write

ANSWERS:

Exercise I: (page 55)	A:	1. 7 2. 5 3. 8 4. 2 5. 6	B:	1. a 2. d 3. c 4. b 5. a	C:	1. b 2. d 3. b 4. d 5. a

Exercise II:
(page 79)

A: 1. 5
2. 2
3. 7
4. 1
5. 5

B: 1. b
2. b
3. d
4. c
5. c

C: 1. noncollegiate
2. progress
3. transatlantic
4. unexpected
5. recalls

Exercise III:
(page 106)

A: 1. 6
2. 4
3. 7
4. 3
5. 1

B: 1. d
2. b
3. b
4. d
5. e

C: 1. b
2. d
3. a
4. c
5. a

Exercise IV:
(page 139)

A: 1. 2 or 6
2. 4
3. 5
4. 2 or 6
5. 7

B: 1. a
2. b
3. f
4. c
5. d

C: 1. *in*gress
2. *e*gress
3. *ag*gressively
4. *con*gress
5. *re*gressing
*pro*gressing

Exercise V:
(page 173)

A: 1. 4
2. 6
3. 1
4. 7
5. 3

B: 1. b
2. a
3. d
4. a
5. a

C: 1. except
2. deposit
3. retain
4. induct
5. emitting

Exercise VI:
(page 199)

A: 1. 3
2. 6
3. 8
4. 2
5. 5

B. 1. a
2. b
3. c
4. d
5. b

C: 1. description
2. feasible
3. attend
4. inspect
5. implied

Exercise VII:
(page 221)

A: 1. 3
2. 7
3. 5
4. 6

B: 1. b
2. a
3. d
4. b

C: 1. status
2. inferred
3. autograph
4. dialogue

Appendix

PRE- *

* See Preface.

94. preprandial
95. pre-Revolution
96. presenile
97. pre-Shakespearean
98. pre-Victorian
99. prevocalic
100. prewar
101. precollege

(*Words having separate entries*)

102. praecocial
103. praecox
104. praedial
105. praefect
106. praelection
107. praemunire
108. praelector
109. praepositor
110. praenomen
111. praenominal
112. praepostor
113. praetexta
114. praetor
115. praetorial
116. praetorian
117. preach
118. preacher
119. preachingly
120. preachify
121. preaching
122. preachment
123. preachy
124. preaxial
125. prebend
126. prebendal
127. prebendary
128. pre-Cambrian
129. precancel
130. precaution
131. precautional
132. precautionary
133. precautious
134. precede
135. precedence
136. precedency
137. precedent
138. precedential

139. preceding
140. precent
141. precentor
142. precentorial
143. precentorship
144. precept
145. preceptive
146. preceptively
147. preceptor
148. preceptoral
149. preceptorial
150. preceptorate
151. preceptory
152. preceptress
153. precession
154. precessional
155. precinct
156. precious
157. preciously
158. preciousness
159. precipice
160. precipitance
161. precipitancy
162. precipitant
163. precipitantly
164. precipitate
165. precipitately
166. precipitateness
167. precipitative
168. precipitator
169. precipitation
170. precipitin
171. precipitous
172. precipitously
173. precipitousness
174. precis
175. precise
176. precisely
177. preciseness
178. precisian
179. precisianism
180. precision
181. precisionist
182. preclinical
183. preclude
184. preclusion
185. preclusive
186. preclusively
187. precocial

188. precocious
189. precociously
190. precociousness
191. precocity
192. preconceive
193. preconception
194. preconcert
195. precondition
196. precognize
197. precritical
198. precursive
199. precursor
200. precursory
201. predate
202. predecease
203. predecessor
204. predesignate
205. predesignation
206. predestinarian
207. predestinarianism
208. predestinate
209. predestination
210. predestine
211. predetermine
212. predetermination
213. predeterminative
214. predial
215. predicable
216. predicability
217. predicableness
218. predicably
219. predicament
220. predicant
221. predicate
222. predication
223. predicative
224. predicatively
225. predicatory
226. predict
227. predictable
228. prediction
229. predictive
230. predictively
231. predictor
232. predigest
233. predigestion
234. predilection
235. predispose
236. predisposition

237. predominance
238. predominancy
239. predominant
240. predominantly
241. predominate
242. predomination
243. predominator
244. preeminence
245. preeminent
246. preeminently
247. preempt
248. preemptive
249. preemptor
250. preemptory
251. preemption
252. preexilian
253. preexilic
254. preexist
255. preexistence
256. preexistent
257. prefabricate
258. prefabrication
259. preface
260. prefatory
261. prefatorily
262. prefect
263. prefecture
264. prefectural
265. prefer
266. preferrer
267. preferable
268. preferability
269. preferableness
270. preferably
271. preference
272. preferential
273. preferentialism
274. preferentialist
275. preferentially
276. preferential shop
277. preferential voting
278. preferment
279. preferred stock
280. prefiguration
281. prefigurative
282. prefigure
283. prefigurement
284. prefix
285. prefixion

286. prefixal
287. prefixally
288. preformation
289. pregnancy
290. pregnant
291. pregnantly
292. prehensile
293. prehensility
294. prehension
295. prehistoric
296. prehistorical
297. prehistory
298. preignition
299. prejudge
300. prejudger
301. prejudgment
302. prejudgement
303. prejudice
304. prejudicial
305. prejudicially
306. prelacy
307. prelate
308. prelatic
309. prelatism
310. prelatist
311. prelature
312. prelect
313. prelection
314. prelector
315. prelibation
316. preliminarily
317. preliminary
318. prelude
319. preluder
320. prelusion
321. prelusive
322. prelusory
323. prelusively
324. prelusorily
325. premature
326. prematurely
327. prematureness
328. prematurity
329. premaxilla
330. premaxillary
331. premedic
332. premedical
333. premeditate
334. premeditative

335. premeditator
336. premeditation
337. premillenarian
338. premillenarianism
339. premillennial
340. premillennialism
341. premillennialist
342. premise
343. premiss
344. premium
345. premolar
346. premonish
347. premonition
348. premonitory
349. premorse
350. prenatal
351. prenatally
352. prenominate
353. prenotion
354. preoccupancy
355. preoccupation
356. preoccupied
357. preoccupy
358. preoral
359. preorally
360. preordain
361. preordination
362. preparation
363. preparative
364. preparator
365. preparatory
366. prepare
367. preparedly
368. preparer
369. preparedness
370. prepay
371. prepayment
372. prepense
373. preponderance
374. preponderant
375. preponderantly
376. preponderate
377. preponderating
378. preponderatingly
379. preponderation
380. preposition
381. prepositional
382. prepositionally
383. prepositive

384. prepositor
385. prepositorial
386. prepossess
387. prepossessingly
388. prepossession
389. preposterous
390. preposterously
391. preposterousness
392. prepostor
393. prepotency
394. prepotent
395. prepotently
396. prepuce
397. preputial
398. pre-Raphaelite
399. pre-Raphaelism
400. prerequisite
401. prerogative
402. prerogative court
403. presage
404. presager
405. preschool
406. prescience
407. prescient
408. presciently
409. prescind
410. prescribe
411. prescriber
412. prescript
413. prescriptible
414. prescription
415. prescriptive
416. prescriptively
417. presence
418. present
419. presentable
420. presentability
421. presentableness
422. presentation
423. presentational
424. presentationism
425. presentationist
426. presentative

427. presentee
428. presenter
429. presentiment
430. presentimental
431. presentive
432. presentively
433. presentiveness
434. presently
435. presentment
436. preservative
437. preserve
438. preservable
439. preservation
440. preserver
441. preside
442. presider
443. presidency
444. president
445. presidential
446. presidentship
447. presidial
448. presidiary
449. presidium
450. presignify
451. prest
452. prestige
453. presume
454. presumable
455. presumably
456. presumedly
457. presumer
458. presumption
459. presumptive
460. presumptively
461. presumptuous
462. presumptuously
463. presumptuousness
464. presuppose
465. presupposition
466. presurmise
467. pretence
468. pretend
469. pretended

470. pretendedly
471. pretender
472. pretense
473. pretension
474. pretentious
475. pretentiously
476. pretentiousness
477. pretext
478. pretor
479. pretorian
480. pretypify
481. prevail
482. prevailing
483. prevailingly
484. prevailingness
485. prevalent
486. prevalence
487. prevalently
488. prevaricate
489. prevarication
490. prevaricator
491. prevenance
492. prevenience
493. prevenient
494. prevent
495. preventable
496. preventible
497. preventer
498. prevention
499. preventative
500. preventive
501. preventively
502. preventiveness
503. preview
504. previous
505. previously
506. previousness
507. previse
508. prevision
509. prevocalic
510. prevocational
511. prevue

Medical words with the prefix *pre-* *

1. preagonal
2. preagonie
3. prealbumin
4. prealbuminuric
5. preanal
6. preanesthetic
7. preantiseptic
8. preaortic
9. preaseptic
10. preataxic
11. preauricular
12. preaxial
13. precancer
14. precancerosis
15. precancerous
16. precapillary
17. precardiac
18. precava
19. precentral
20. prechordal
21. precipitant
22. precipitinogen
23. precipitogen
24. precipitinogenoid
25. precipitoid
26. precipitophore
27. precipitum
28. preclival
29. precommissure
30. preconscious
31. preconvulsive
32. precordia
33. precordial
34. precordialgia
35. precordium
36. precornu
37. precostal
38. precuneal
39. precuneate
40. precuneus
41. precunial
42. predentin
43. prediabetes
44. prediastole
45. prediastolic
46. predicrotic
47. prednisolone

48. prednisone
49. prednisteroid
50. predormitium
51. preeclampisa
52. preepiglottic
53. preeruptive
54. prefontal
55. preganglionic
56. pregnane
57. pregnanediol
58. pregnanedione
59. pregnene
60. pregneniolone
61. pregnenolone
62. prehallux
63. prehemiplegic
64. prehyoid
65. prehypophysis
66. preinduction
67. preinsula
68. prelacrimal
69. prelaryngeal
70. prelimbic
71. prelum
72. premalignant
73. premaniacal
74. premedication
75. premenstrual
76. premenstruum
77. premorbid
78. premunition
79. premunitive
80. premyloblast
81. premyelocyte
82. prenarcosis
83. prenaris
84. prenares
85. preneoplastic
86. preoperative
87. preoperculum
88. preoptic
89. preopticus
90. preoral
91. prepalatal
92. prepallium
93. preparalytic
94. prepatellar

95. prepeduncle
96. preperforatum
97. preperitoneal
98. preptian
99. preplacental
100. prepontile
101. prepuberal
102. prepubertal
103. prepubescent
104. preputial
105. preputium
106. prepyloric
107. prepyramidal
108. preramus
109. prerectal
110. prerenal
111. prereproductive
112. presacral
113. presecretion
114. presenile
115. presenility
116. presobase
117. presphygmic
118. prespinal
119. prespondylolostheses
120. presternum
121. presuppurative
122. presylvian
123. presystole
124. pretarsal
125. prethyroid
126. prethyroideal
127. prethroidean
128. pretibial
129. pretoxemia
130. pretympanic
131. preurethritis
132. prevenception
133. preventorium
134. prevermis
135. prevertebral
136. prevertiginous
137. prevesical
138. prezone
139. presymogen

* From *Stedman's Medical Dictionary*, 20th ed., The Williams & Wilkins Co., 1961. Includes only those words *not* listed in the collegiate dictionary.